100 Ideas for Secondary Teachers:
Student Personal Development

Kelly Allchin

BLOOMSBURY EDUCATION
LONDON OXFORD NEW YORK NEW DELHI SYDNEY

BLOOMSBURY EDUCATION
Bloomsbury Publishing Plc
50 Bedford Square, London, WC1B 3DP, UK
Bloomsbury Publishing Ireland Limited
29 Earlsfort Terrace, Dublin 2, D02 AY28, Ireland

BLOOMSBURY, BLOOMSBURY EDUCATION and the Diana logo are
trademarks of Bloomsbury Publishing Plc

First published in Great Britain, 2025 by Bloomsbury Publishing Plc
This edition published in Great Britain, 2025 by Bloomsbury Publishing Plc

Text copyright © Kelly Allchin, 2025

Kelly Allchin has asserted her right under the Copyright, Designs
and Patents Act, 1988, to be identified as Author of this work

Bloomsbury Publishing Plc does not have any control over, or responsibility for, any third-party websites referred to or in this book. All internet addresses given in this book were correct at the time of going to press. The author and publisher regret any inconvenience caused if addresses have changed or sites have ceased to exist, but can accept no responsibility for any such changes

Every effort has been made to trace copyright holders and to obtain their permission for the use of copyright material. The publisher apologises for any errors or omissions and would be grateful if notified of any corrections that should be incorporated in future reprints or editions of this book

All rights reserved. No part of this publication may be: i) reproduced or transmitted in any form, electronic or mechanical, including photocopying, recording or by means of any information storage or retrieval system without prior permission in writing from the publishers; or ii) used or reproduced in any way for the training, development or operation of artificial intelligence (AI) technologies, including generative AI technologies. The rights holders expressly reserve this publication from the text and data mining exception as per Article 4(3) of the Digital Single Market Directive (EU) 2019/790.

A catalogue record for this book is available from the British Library

ISBN: PB: 978-1-8019-9461-3; ePDF: 978-1-8019-9460-6;
ePub: 978-1-8019-9459-0

2 4 6 8 10 9 7 5 3 1 (paperback)

Typeset by Newgen KnowledgeWorks Pvt. Ltd., Chennai, India
Printed and bound in the UK by CPI Group Ltd, CR0 4YY

MIX
Paper | Supporting
responsible forestry
FSC® C013604

To find out more about our authors and books visit www.bloomsbury.com
and sign up for our newsletters

For product safety related questions contact
productsafety@bloomsbury.com

Contents

Acknowledgements	vi
Introduction	vii
How to use this book	ix

Part 1: Curriculum — **1**
1. Where to start? — 2
2. Developing expert teams — 4
3. Cross-curricular PSHE links — 5
4. Effective form time delivery — 6
5. Data-informed curriculum — 7
6. Drop-down days — 8
7. The whole school body — 10
8. Pro-active and re-active — 11

Part 2: Student leadership — **13**
9. You said, we did! — 14
10. Student-led surgeries — 15
11. Peer coaching – one-to-one behaviour — 16
12. Self-esteem building — 18
13. Curriculum coaching — 19
14. Personalised parliament — 20
15. Accrediting student leaders — 21
16. Hotspots — 22
17. Online organisation — 23
18. Staff recruitment — 24

Part 3: Community and social action — **25**
19. Deciding on a school charity — 26
20. Purposeful fundraising — 27
21. Food bank — 28
22. Awareness stalls — 29
23. Community gratitude — 30
24. Little Free Library — 31
25. Community computing — 32
26. Primary helpers — 33
27. Community club — 34

Part 4: Careers education — **35**
28. Real models vs role models — 36
29. Flat pack team building hack — 37
30. My life at 30 — 38
31. Careers in the curriculum — 39
32. Future learning — 40
33. Developing professional relationships — 42
34. Sector experience days — 43
35. I'll tell you what I want... — 44
36. Breaking stereotypes — 45
37. LMI, why? — 46
38. The early signs – NEET — 47

Part 5: Mental health and wellbeing — **49**
39. Wellbeing pack — 50
40. What's behind the door? — 51
41. Student health and wellbeing charter — 52
42. Staff health and wellbeing charter — 53
43. Who does what, and so what? — 54
44. Wellbeing digital wall — 55
45. Ask It Basket – next generation! — 56
46. KS4 and KS5 transition — 57
47. Being mindful of mindfulness — 58
48. Friendship club — 59

Part 6: Form time and assembly — **61**
49. Why? — 62
50. Assembly calendar — 64
51. Culture assemblies — 65
52. Who's who? — 66
53. What do you think about that then? — 67
54. Form time notices — 68
55. Check in, check out! — 69
56. Form identity — 70
57. British values and assemblies — 71
58. Birthday bonanza! — 72

Part 7: PSHE ideas — **73**
59. Writing on tables — 74
60. Distancing techniques — 75
61. Coulda, shoulda, woulda — 76
62. Safeguarding against triggering content — 77
63. The power of opting out — 78
64. Establishing ground rules — 79

65	Reading in form time	80
66	Shock tactics: wrong tactics!	82
67	Educating or glamourising?	83
68	University links	84
69	Recording learning	85

Part 8: Citizenship ideas — **87**

70	Camera project	88
71	Developing political literacy	90
72	School surgery	91
73	Citizenship in the wider curriculum	92
74	Human rights club	93
75	Active citizenship	94
76	Human rights as a hook	95
77	Debate academy	96
78	Five newspapers, one day	98
79	Engaging with power	99
80	Me map!	100

Part 9: Quality assurance — **101**

81	What does the data say?	102
82	Assessing the right things	103
83	Case studies	104
84	External verification	105
85	Market research	106
86	Supporting non-specialists	107
87	Fact-checking and relevance	108
88	Positively inclusive PSHE	109
89	Let's talk about sex! (Unless we can't?)	110
90	Vetting external agencies	112
91	Evidencing your PD via data	113

Part 10: Whole-school approaches — **115**

92	Knock, knock	116
93	Wall of fame	117
94	Yours sincerely	118
95	PD parent evenings	119
96	Parent support group	120
97	Shout about it!	121
98	PD student score	122
99	Supporting new students	124
100	Policy makers	125

Acknowledgements

A huge thank you to Joanna Ramsay from Bloomsbury, who listened to my ideas many moons ago and guided me through the process to get those initial ideas into print. Also, to both Joanna and Cathy Lear for their support and guidance through the editing process – editors are magicians!

Thank you to the amazing staff and students at Leeds City Academy. In this most wonderful school, my love, experience and passion for personal development had the chance to grow due to the freedom and autonomy given to me. You will always have a special place in my heart.

To my parents, Mick and Sandra. Your unconditional belief in my abilities and support through college and university have been the bedrock of everything I have achieved to date and I am forever grateful.

Finally, to my little squad. My gorgeous family, Ben, Eleni and Willow. Thank you Ben for backing my decisions 100% and pushing me to follow my heart. My girls, you are my motivation for everything and I love you completely.

Introduction

When we think about schools being a place for education, our thoughts often naturally gravitate to the academic. It is, after all, indisputable that student academic outcomes are important – they are the passport to students' next stage of education, training or employment.

But education is so much more than that.

Schools have always played a crucial role in developing the whole child: teaching the importance of respect, exploring skills and qualities, and encouraging aspirational thinking. The introduction of personal development as a part of the inspection framework has now placed this vital area of education firmly centre stage.

It invites schools to carefully consider the holistic education of their students and go beyond the academic by doing things such as:

- developing students' emotional intelligence, self-awareness and sense of personal character
- supporting students in setting goals, thinking carefully about the type of life they want for themselves and how they can get there
- developing an understanding of democracy, justice and civic responsibility so that they can contribute positively to society.

Personal development shouldn't sit in a silo. It can develop resilience and critical thinking, which supports students in their academic lessons. It teaches the importance of organisation and develops responsibility, supporting attendance. Emotional intelligence is nurtured, which can benefit relationships throughout the school, which in turn positively impacts behaviour.

The framework exists to support the whole student and, when done well, should be the golden thread that runs through your school ethos.

The ideas in this book have been written with a diverse audience in mind. Since the changes to the inspection framework took place, many teachers and school leaders have taken on additional responsibilities in leading this huge area, some of whom may have a strong background in leading PSHE or similar and some of whom are coming to the role as novices. I hope that there are ideas here to support everyone, both in terms of the nitty gritty, such as planning your curriculum and personalising your offer, and in terms of providing lots of innovative ideas to elevate your offer to the next level.

Personal development within a school are exciting and hugely rewarding, but it's a mammoth area too, so take your time, build up slowly, keep your students at the core of your decision-making, and most of all, enjoy it!

I'd love to hear any stories about your personal development journey. Contact me via @smscallchin on X (formerly known as Twitter).

How to use this book

This book includes simple, practical, tried-and-tested ideas to equip every personal development lead to confidently assess and improve their personal development offer, from classroom ideas to whole-school approaches.

Each idea includes:

- a catchy title, easy to refer to and share with your colleagues
- an interesting quote linked to the idea
- a summary of the idea in bold, making it easy to flick through the book and identify an idea you want to use at a glance
- a step-by-step guide to implementing the idea.

Each idea also includes one or more of the following:

Teaching tip

Practical tips and advice for how and how not to run the activity or put the idea into practice.

Taking it further

Ideas and advice for how to extend the idea or develop it further.

Bonus idea ★

There are 18 Bonus ideas in this book that are extra-exciting, extra-original and extra-interesting.

Share how you use these ideas and find out what other practitioners have done using **#100ideas**.

Online resources for this book can be found at: bloomsbury.pub/100-ideas-SPD

Curriculum

Part 1

IDEA 1

Where to start?

'I haven't got a clue where to begin!'

The range of personal development is huge, covering PSHE, RSE, student leadership, health and wellbeing, character education, cultural capital, citizenship, British values, careers education and much more. Just getting started can feel like a big task — here's how to do it in a manageable way.

Teaching tip

Networking is vital. If you haven't already, create an X account (formerly Twitter) and start following lots of PD leads. @PDNetworkUK is a great one to begin with.

There are lots of exciting things that a personal development (PD) lead can get their teeth stuck into, but be sure to keep it doable. When putting together your PD programme, think quality not quantity and start small. Be forensic when planning each stage, gather the student and staff voice, and use data to inform you (see **Idea 81**). Observe how things are going, make necessary tweaks, and only then move on to the next stage. If you're not careful, PD can get out of hand, and you find you are doing lots of 'stuff' but with no strategy behind it.

Ensure you know the RSE statutory guidance, and aim to get this in place first — this book has many ideas on how to deliver this element. If planning for this is overwhelming, explore 'off-the-shelf options', and join the PSHE Association to access their resources. Nothing is stopping you from creating your own resources, but this doesn't have to be done from the start.

Likewise, students have an entitlement to receive impartial career advice and guidance, so ensuring you have a Level 6 qualified careers lead in place is crucial. You could look to add capacity to this area by 'growing your own' — do you have any staff who would be willing to take the Level 4 qualification as a part of their professional development? There are also numerous organisations where you can outsource one-to-one career interviews, and this might be worth exploring if you are not yet in a position to provide this in house.

Familiarise yourself with what is included within British values (you will find there is a lot of crossover with citizenship) and ensure the values are actively promoted. Assembly time is an easy way to introduce these values to students and explore their importance.
This will have greater impact than a poster in a classroom.

Once you have the above in place, you can then look to build capacity and improve quality. Think of the initial stages as the 'bones' of your PD offer, which will become fleshed out into something personalised and high quality over time. The rest will come – don't rush it!

> **Bonus idea** ★
>
> Reach out to other schools. If you're in a Trust, use them; if you're in a cluster of schools, ask for support. There will be lots of experienced PD leads who will be able to talk through how they approach their role or to share resources. But don't try to replicate everything they do – this is about gaining advice and creating a sounding board.

IDEA 2

Developing expert teams

'I get to teach the bits I like.'

In many schools, form tutors deliver PSHE content to tutees. This can be a positive approach and help foster tutor/tutee relationships. This idea also avoids the issue of tutors needing to be experts on the whole PSHE curriculum.

Delivering PSHE content is challenging due to the amount of new knowledge to learn, as well as the sensitive topics involved. This idea shakes things up by rotating the form time teams. Each member of the form tutor team becomes an expert in one area of PSHE, and delivers this topic to a group of students over a term. They then rotate to teach the same content to a different group, and so on. The core curriculum still needs to be planned and distributed centrally, but this is a different way to deliver it.

Keep things simple by using the PSHE Association's core themes of Health and Wellbeing, Relationships, and Living in the Wider World. This allows a termly or half-termly rotation and gives each area equal weighting.

Carry out staff voice to determine who would prefer to teach what. You might decide to link this with obvious subject similarities, e.g. by having the maths team deliver finance education, but don't become limited by this – allow some choice. Consider opening this up to support staff too: this will make the approach truly whole school and will also make logistics easier in terms of staff numbers and rotations. For logistical ease (to make rotation simpler), you need three core teams for each year group.

Once you have divided staff into core teams, this will also make continuing professional development (CPD) easier, more efficient and personalised to what staff will be teaching.

> **Bonus idea** ★
>
> If you are worried about losing the 'core tutor' element of PSHE, keep form time as normal, with standard tutor groups on Mondays and Fridays (see **Idea 55**), and PSHE delivered on the remaining days.

IDEA 3

Cross-curricular PSHE links

'Mapping PSHE this way allowed us to see what could be covered within wider curricula.'

Discrete PSHE lessons are vital for ensuring breadth of coverage and time to reflect, discuss and demonstrate key skills. But if time is tight, think about natural links to other subjects so PSHE can also be covered in the wider curriculum. Here are some ideas.

Lots of the content around health and wellbeing-related decisions, drugs and alcohol, and managing risk can be covered via your science curriculum. With such a large crossover with science, you could consider having one week per year where science holds a 'PSHE takeover' week and delves deeper into the science topics with PSHE crossover.

Positive relationships lend themselves well to English literature. Work with your English department to choose a text to study that meets the needs of their curriculum whilst allowing meaningful discussions of healthy and unhealthy relationships.

Financial education has clear links to maths, so when working with percentages link this to loans and investments, and use real numerical data to explore the cost of living.

Computing will offer many opportunities to teach digital resilience.

If your school also adopts a 'careers in the curriculum' model (see **Idea 31**) this will also support many of the careers and pathways elements of your PSHE curriculum.

Remember, with this approach, you are not trying to teach all of PSHE through the wider curriculum; instead, you are identifying clear links and making the most of these.

Teaching tip

As well as ensuring separate departments have PSHE links included in their curriculum, create an online shared area where this cross-curricular approach is evidenced. Include example lessons, photos of students' work, and how and when these lessons are taught.

IDEA 4

Effective form time delivery

'If you only have 30 minutes, every minute needs to count!'

If your school uses form time to deliver the bulk of your PD programme, it's important you think carefully about how best to utilise the short amount of time available.

Teaching tip

Think carefully about how you will incorporate signposting into your sequence. You may wish to drip-feed this throughout, teach it explicitly during Session 1, or provide students with a physical resource that they can take away.

Planning a 30-minute session is not the same as planning for an hour. Students don't have the time to acquire knowledge and practise in the same way, so be creative with delivery and think about the learning as a sequence that is developed over the week, rather than something to be achieved in a single session.

If working on the premise that your PSHE delivery takes up three form time slots a week (at least this amount is recommended if this forms the bulk of your delivery) try planning your content via three-part sequences of learning, where each week a new topic is examined. For example:

- **Session 1: Teacher instruction** – students learn about it. This element is very knowledge-based – students are taught key facts and correct definitions are explored.
- **Session 2: Discussion** – students explore the topic via discussion. This could be via agree/disagree statements, card sorts or similar.
- **Session 3: Scenario/case study work** – students demonstrate their skills. Students discuss a case study relating to what they have learned, exploring what the characters could do or how they may be feeling (see **Idea 60**).

IDEA 5

Data-informed curriculum

'Why do you teach that specific topic then, and in that way?'

Think flexibly when deciding how to order and prioritise different elements of your PD programme.

Once you are confident you are delivering the statutory content, think creatively about how and when you cover the rest.

The wider PSHE curriculum should be data-driven (see **Idea 81**). Do certain topics need to come forward or do you need to spend longer on others? For example, if your data suggests that only 5 per cent of your students have tried alcohol, but that 40 per cent have tried a vape, this will inform lesson allocation. Or if a very small number of students are applying for apprenticeships, is this an informed choice, or did they receive information about this route too late? If attendance drops off towards the end of term, could this be the time to launch some of your exciting PD work?

If developing peer-coaching programmes, don't be set in stone regarding the year groups that take part, but be informed by what your behavioural data is saying, as the need could change. Likewise, look at your sign-up data for general student leadership groups. Is there equity amongst key cohorts? If not, why not? Look at how and when these opportunities are launched to ensure key groups aren't disadvantaged.

When are your students attending extracurricular clubs? Which are the most popular? Look to adapt your offer to provide more of what they love (whilst still keeping other opportunities open) and explore when clubs take place to encourage attendance.

Teaching tip

If something isn't working, do some research to try and find out why. There is so much data available within a school, so use it!

IDEA 6

Drop-down days

'There's a real buzz about the day!'

Invite external organisations to support elements of your PSHE content via drop-down days. With this model, you are getting specialist delivery and immersing students into PSHE topics, plus you don't have to worry about staff delivering content they're not comfortable with.

Teaching tip

Ensure that students are still safeguarded against triggering content, just like you would within a traditional PSHE model, and make sure all external sessions have been quality assured (see **Idea 62**: Safeguarding against triggering content and **Idea 90**: Vetting external agencies).

Drop-down days offer many benefits. Here are some tips to help you make the most of them.

Mapping and forward-thinking are key. Drop-down themes need to be mapped in advance and organisations booked months ahead to ensure your students get the content you intended. Once you are happy with your mapping, keep to this model. This means that when facilitators visit, you can secure the next year's booking before they leave! Over time they will start to get to know you and your students – and you might even be able to negotiate a reduced rate.

Student tracking is vital. If you are using drop-down days to deliver statutory PSHE content, you will need a clear policy that states what happens if a student is absent. Keep spreadsheets that show students who were present and received the content, as well as absent students, with an outline of the steps you made to ensure they didn't miss out on statutory content. Add this to your calendar of events, e.g. if a drop-down day takes place in early November, plan a mop-up session in late November.

If planning a relationships and sex education-themed drop-down day, think ahead to ensure students who have been withdrawn from sex education still have a high-quality educational offer. Liaise with the organisation so you're clear as to which aspects cover sex (meaning that those students will need to be withdrawn) and ensure an alternative offer is put in place for any students impacted.

Make sure students have the opportunity to digest what they have learned at a later date. Plan for this by creating a small workbook for each year group based on the external sessions they have taken part in. This could include a recap of factual knowledge, some reflection questions and, most importantly, a reminder of signposting for where to go for further information. These could be completed during form time after the drop-down day. These require minimal teacher input and are very much student-led.

Taking it further

This approach can be expensive – work with your senior leadership team (SLT) to ensure you are clear about budgets so you can prioritise who to book. Also reach out to your local authority PSHE teams to see what they can offer.

IDEA 7

The whole school body

'Our staff give us an insight as to what our students might need.'

Personal development can sometimes feel quite insular as it is often run by very few staff members. Use a survey to get input from the whole staff body and avoid it being you alone who comes up with all the ideas and answers.

Taking it further

Set up a PD focus group, and ask if any staff members would be willing to meet to discuss the answers in more detail. This will allow you to unpick anything of interest.

An effective PD programme aims to develop positive character traits in all of our students, to support them at school and beyond. So who better to ask than your full staff body?

This idea isn't designed to get you to re-evaluate your whole PD programme as a result of what school staff have commented on – you are the expert. Instead, this idea raises things you may not have seen yourself.

Think carefully about what you want to find out, e.g. which school values are students demonstrating the most/least? Are students demonstrating good manners? Which current affairs topics are students discussing? Which aspects of self-esteem are supporting/hindering students in class?

Formulate a simple online survey where staff can input simple quantitative answers, as well as longer qualitative answers. Ensure the survey includes an introduction about why you are doing this and the impact you hope it will have.

Send the survey out to *all* staff, not just teaching staff. If you're looking for information about students' characters and behaviours, you want to ask everyone. Ask your headteacher if they would be willing to mention the importance of this questionnaire in a staff briefing or the headteacher bulletin.

Once the answers are in, use them to inform how you deliver personal development.

IDEA 8

Pro-active and re-active

'It can be so hard to get the balance right.'

It can be tricky to keep to your PSHE curriculum, as when something happens nationally or in your local community you may want to drop everything and discuss it. Likewise, if there is a safeguarding incident you may wish to address it within PSHE.

Although it makes sense to do this, there also needs to be caution and meticulous tracking of the content being covered. PSHE time is often limited. If it's chopped into regularly, you can find that chunks of the curriculum are being lost or that lesson progression stalls.

First, ensure that your PSHE curriculum clearly tracks statutory content. Towards the end of each half term review this documentation to be sure that these sessions went ahead. If they were missed, these are what need to be prioritised during the next half term to ensure you are meeting your statutory obligations.

If you have discrete PSHE lessons or form time, keep to the curriculum within these and use assemblies for reactive content. This ensures that the curriculum is followed but that you have the attention of all students when an immediate issue needs to be discussed.

If your school marks key events, e.g. Anti-Bullying Week, map these within your PSHE curriculum so they are in sync. This way they are celebrated and enhance your already planned content, rather than replacing it.

Another option is to introduce 'What's going on Wednesday?' in the weeks where it is needed. The safeguarding team or PSHE lead creates a simple slide that contains key information and signposts support. Likewise, this could be in the form of a short pre-recorded video.

> **Bonus idea** ★
>
> Staff are used to receiving bulletins, but what about students? Create a simple design for an online student bulletin and populate this as and when needed. This could include important information and signposting, and be emailed to all students to access in their own time.

Part 2

Student leadership

IDEA 9

You said, we did!

'I haven't got a clue what our school council actually does.'

Effective student leadership groups, be that a school council or student parliament, need to have 'representation' at their core. The whole student body must see this group as a vehicle to voice their ideas, concerns and general thoughts.

Having a 'you said, we did' display board in a central location is a great way of celebrating how your student leadership group listens to and acts on the feedback they receive from their peers.

Pick a central location for your display board. Ideally, this should also be a place where students can pause and read the information, e.g. the school canteen, student reception or even near the student toilets.

The board should display, in a clear and simple-to-read way, what the student leadership group is currently working on and why. Visually, having the text for 'you said' in large speech bubbles and 'we did' in large stars works well.

The board needs updating regularly (this should be the responsibility of the students) to keep it current. Include progress photos or information about what's coming next.

Ensure that school staff, in particular school leaders, are aware of the content going on the board. This is a literal representation of what your student body wants and needs, so staff need to engage with this and offer their ideas. This will hugely support the student leadership group to be effective.

> **Bonus idea** ★
>
> Consider having a suggestion box next to the display board – this is a great way for the wider student body to engage with student leadership.

IDEA 10

Student-led surgeries

'Time to meet my representative.'

Student leadership groups are a fantastic way to develop their political literacy and understanding of democracy.

In a school setting, student-led surgeries provide the same opportunities as 'real life' constituency surgeries. Students can meet and chat with the peers who represent them, voicing their ideas and concerns.

The importance of representation needs to be made absolutely clear throughout your election process. Surgeries won't work if student leaders view themselves alone as the people making core decisions. They must understand that their role is to represent the collective views of the student body, including students they might not know or have much in common with.

Surgeries should take place in large, open and safe spaces that all students can access, e.g. libraries. They need to be advertised well and timetabled so that any student can attend – lunchtimes work well. With this in mind, you may need to alternate the days that your surgeries take place. Students may have clubs on certain days, so alternating helps attendance.

Have processes to manage the number of students attending so surgeries are viable for all. For example, set days for certain years, use a sign-up sheet (similar to parent evenings) or run group surgeries where two student leaders meet ten peers. Put a time limit on each meeting – egg timers work well, allowing both parties to see how much time remains.

Develop a simple way to record ideas, such as pairing up student leaders, so that one speaks with their peers whilst the other makes notes.

Teaching tip

It's vital that students summarise and share what has been discussed. Surgeries cannot become tokenistic, or students will simply stop attending.

IDEA 11

Peer coaching – one-to-one behaviour

'My coach helped me to see the type of person I could be.'

Peer influence is huge during adolescence. Although adults can still have an impact, for many teenagers, the people they look to for guidance, approval and support are other teenagers.

Teaching tip

Behind the scenes, the coachee's behaviour must be tracked. Where appropriate (following safeguarding guidelines) share with coaches their coachee's successes and setbacks, so that these can be acknowledged.

By establishing a peer-coaching programme, you are ensuring your students have positive peer relationships to draw upon and providing positive role models at a time in students' lives when these things are at their most important.

To ensure that coachees can 'look up' to and have an element of trust and respect towards their coach, a model where Years 10 and 11 coach Years 7 and 8 works well. Ultimately, this will depend on your individual cohorts and what your behavioural data is telling you. You may want to put all your focus into a particular year group, or even a particular cohort. You are best placed to make that initial decision.

Advertise the programme to the year groups who have the opportunity to apply for the coaching positions. Ideally, this should be during an assembly so that all students get the message and understand the importance of the programme.

Clearly communicate your specification for applying, and the rationale for this. I set the non-negotiables as:

- a genuine want to help others
- good attendance (they need to be there!)
- good punctuality.

You aren't necessarily looking for a perfect behaviour record but with a less consistent one there needs to have been an improvement.

Sometimes, the best coaches are the older students who made mistakes in lower school but – importantly – have learned from these. This lived experience is hugely valuable, so don't discount those students.

Ensure you have an accessible sign-up or application process. There needs to be something formal in place so students can show commitment. Literacy shouldn't be a barrier to applying, so consider using form tutor referrals as well as written applications.

Once you have selected your coaches, each coach needs to be matched to a coachee. Do not rush this stage; use data to inform you and think about personalities. It works best when done in collaboration, such as the head of Year 8 working with the head of Year 11.

Whilst this is taking place, train your coaches. The training will depend on your students but should include time to reflect on why they applied, develop empathy, consider the types of conversations they could have with their coachee, and how they will motivate and encourage the coachee. If there is time, allowing the year manager of the coachees some time with the coaches to discuss their students is beneficial.

Once coaches and coachees have been matched, it's time for them to meet. Going straight into one-to-one conversations is intense, so start as a group. Place four or five pairs into a larger group and let them hang out in a relaxed way – card games and snacks help!

Once everyone is more relaxed, the students can work in pairs. Dedicate a form time session for this each week, where students can come to a communal space to chat about their week – the library works well for this. You could also provide coaches with their coachee's timetable and give them specific times in the week when they are allowed a 10-minute pass to check on their coachee. This approach is highly effective but must be agreed upon as a whole staff body.

> **Taking it further**
>
> It's vital to check in regularly with the coaches – they will often become highly invested in their coachees and feel bad if they can't see an impact. Remind them that impact isn't always visible, but that they are playing a key role in providing a positive influence to their coachee.

IDEA 12

Self-esteem building

'My coaches helped me to feel more confident and happy at school.'

Despite our best efforts, sometimes Year 7 students will find secondary school daunting. Small group self-esteem coaching with caring older students is a lovely way to build confidence.

Teaching tip

Help coaches to design a pre- and post-programme questionnaire for their coachees. This will help you and them to measure impact.

This coaching idea is focused on supporting Year 7 students with their confidence and self-esteem and is therefore best suited to coaches who have naturally caring and calm personalities, as they will be working with students who will likely be feeling shy or nervous.

Small group coaching is structured. With support from a member of staff, coaches will work together, to plan and deliver a fun-filled 6-week form time programme to develop each student's self-confidence.

The sessions should be student-led but with staff support. Book a welcoming space for these sessions to take place, e.g. a meeting room or the library. Groups of ten work well, with four or five coaches to five or six coachees. The suggested 6-week programme could include:

- 'Getting to know you' session– provide board games, and snacks!
- More games and gentle discussions about likes and dislikes.
- Conversation cards open discussion – coaches can make these themselves.
- Self-esteem word search – coaches make a word search with positive adjectives about their coachees.
- 'All About Me' posters – coaches help their coachees to create these, ensuring the poster highlights their qualities.
- Presentation of posters (this can be very low-key) and celebration.

IDEA 13

Curriculum coaching

'It was like a lightbulb had been switched on – they finally got it!'

Sometimes, for a student to understand a tricky concept, they need to hear it explained in a different way, away from the classroom. This is where curriculum coaches can help. Pairing up students who are highly confident and skilled in a particular area of the curriculum with students who need a bit more support can have a positive impact on both the coach and coachee.

This is not about taking the responsibility for progress away from teachers who are the experts in the classroom. This idea offers additional support and is still very much teacher-led.

Start small with one subject department. Willingness is key as this idea will rely on information and support from the subject lead and teachers. The subject team should discuss crucial curriculum areas that students find difficult to grasp, deciding on two or three to focus on.

Identify and approach students who have proved through assessment that they understand these areas well. Curriculum coaching should be introduced to them as a leadership opportunity that could further consolidate their understanding.

Teachers need to be specific about what they want the coach to support with, but not overly prescriptive. Provide a sounding board and ensure coaches can talk their ideas through and request resources.

Once the coach has spent time with their coachee, the teacher should reflect on the coachee's progress using formal or informal assessment methods.

Teaching tip

Think about when the coaching will take place and how much time is needed. It's counterproductive to take students out of lessons so consider utilising the form period. Another option is to run this as an optional afterschool intervention.

IDEA 14

Personalised parliament

'Our student parliament is the absolute opposite of tokenistic – they feed directly into school improvement.'

Many schools have a student parliament or similar. This idea helps to directly link the work of student leadership groups with what the SLT and wider leadership groups are trying to achieve.

Taking it further

Ensure the school calendar includes half-termly full parliament meetings. These should be an opportunity for each department to share their manifestos and actions, seek support and ideas, and celebrate success. Ideally these should also be attended by the school principal.

Launch the student parliament at the same time as school leaders are finalising their school improvement plan. This ensures student leadership directly feeds into school improvement and the impact is clear.

Consider having different departments within your parliament. This serves two purposes: it mimics government and so is great for political literacy; and it allows for greater variety, as students have more options to get involved in different areas of school life.

A simple structure is to have a department linked to each area of school leadership, which can then be overseen by the link member of the SLT, such as quality of education, behaviour, etc. Include departments that represent whole-school priorities, such as wellbeing, attendance or safeguarding. The point is to personalise your student parliament to what your school is trying to achieve as a collective.

Each department then creates a manifesto. Students should have access to a student-friendly version of the school improvement plan that links to their department area. The manifesto should be SMART and include lots of opportunities for whole-school opinion-seeking and collaboration. This model will ensure that the student voice is genuinely considered when making school decisions and writing policy.

IDEA 15

Accrediting student leaders

'Our students gained so much from being developed as leaders, but giving them an actual accreditation was the icing on the cake.'

Providing student leadership opportunities is excellent because of the skills that are developed as a result. Being a school leader develops confidence, improves communication, allows for strategic thinking, and allows young people to see themselves as changemakers.

Accreditation shouldn't be the driving reason for setting up student leadership streams, but it is an avenue to be explored. If you have existing well-managed and effective leadership streams, why not look into accreditation as a bonus?

Start small and consider looking to accredit one of the streams – ideally one that is well-established and has a track record of success.

Accreditation must be planned in the same way that a curriculum lead plans for final assessments: there needs to be a clear plan, well-communicated success criteria, deadlines that students must meet to submit evidence and a robust moderation process.

Consider joining the Schools, Students and Teachers (SSAT) network to access their student leadership accreditation. They grade their work using a self-assessment framework that covers ten core skill sets grouped into three themes: developing myself; working with others; and contributing to my community.

The ILM Young Leaders Award is a nationally recognised qualification that is also worth exploring. Schools have the option to deliver the award in-house or use ILM's specialist leadership training providers.

Taking it further

For leadership accreditation to be handled effectively and purposefully evaluated, it will need a member of staff to have oversight. Consider advertising this as a PD role within the school, offering a small bursary or allowing additional planning, preparation and assessment time (PPA) time for a teacher to complete the work.

IDEA 16

Hotspots

'Actually being able to see the areas in the school where students felt less safe helped us to be proactive in our safeguarding approach.'

Ensuring that students feel safe is crucial for their PD, but here's how to ensure that what we think is the reality. As school staff, we are viewing the school through the eyes of an adult, which is likely to be very different to how a student sees things.

Teaching tip

Ensure that all completed maps are seen by a member of staff to check for any safeguarding issues that might be missed by student leaders.

This is a great activity to complete with your whole student body via the student leadership groups, who can then work with school leaders to develop and implement an action plan.

Students need to feel safe and comfortable to complete this activity honestly. So group students together with peers they feel comfortable with – this is an activity where working with a friend might be of benefit. Keep groups small as everyone must have their say.

Print out multiple copies of your school floor plan, ideally in black and white on A3 paper so that there's enough room to make notes around the sides. Each group of students should have a copy of the map and green and red pens. Before starting the activity, ensure that students understand the map – talk them through it so that there are no errors!

Ask students to discuss where in school they feel safe and unsafe, highlighting areas that feel particularly safe in green, and unsafe in red. Encourage them to provide brief explanations, and make stating their names optional.

Once this has been completed, student leaders should compile the maps and comments and produce a summary presentation to share with the SLT. School leaders and senior leaders can then work together to carry out smaller, more focused group work and create an action plan.

IDEA 17

Online organisation

'Keeping our student leadership groups organised was a bit of a nightmare; it now feels much more manageable.'

Student leadership groups can be tricky to organise as they are often made up of students from different year groups, who all have lots of ideas they want to share. Communicating information about meetings, sharing key information and setting actions can feel like a full-time job in itself, so make things easier by keeping this all together via an online platform.

Having an online platform doesn't replace face-to-face meetings, but it can make your meeting time more efficient as the bulk of the administration has already been sorted. It also develops important life skills – online platforms are used in a wide range of career settings, so it's good to get your student leaders used to this way of collaborative working whilst in school.

Use the same online platform that your students are already used to, such as Google Classrooms or Microsoft Teams, and set up a group area for each separate student leadership group within school.

Within each group area, organise the space into sections for agendas, minutes and ideas. Use the calendar to let students know about upcoming meetings (no more trying to get messages out in form!). You can also use the area to post links to articles or videos that your student leadership group might find interesting.

Taking it further

Managing your student leadership online platform is a role that could be shared amongst the students themselves. Encourage the students to take minutes and upload them and to use the space to communicate key leadership messages with each other.

IDEA 18

Staff recruitment

'Our students play a crucial role in the process.'

If you already involve students in staff recruitment, take this further and use it as a genuine opportunity to develop their skills.

Taking it further

If you don't want to be limited to just using these students during interviews, then don't be. The training they have received should ensure that they are well-equipped to support other students with getting involved.

Rather than giving students questions to ask new candidates, why not have them be involved in creating the questions? Rather than always using the same few trusted students to interview candidates, open the opportunity up to the wider student body.

Consider adding staff recruitment as a specific branch within your student leadership structure. Advertise and recruit for this in the same way that you would any other leadership opportunity so that students know what it's all about and can decide whether it would be good for them.

This group must be representative of the whole student body, so be aware of this when advertising and use your pastoral teams to support you in raising the role's profile amongst key groups. Make it clear to students that you want the group to be representative.

Aim for 3–4 students from each year group, and meet with them to ensure they understand their role in the recruitment process. This is great for them as it develops their leadership skills and knowledge, and it's also great for you as you are bringing experience to this area of student leadership. Set the students up with a group email address to make communication and the sharing of information easier.

You now have a core team trained in all elements of recruitment to call upon when there is recruitment coming up, who will be, so should be good to go at relatively short notice.

Part 3

Community and social action

IDEA 19

Deciding on a school charity

'It's great to hear them so passionate about their chosen charity.'

Students love a fundraiser! Especially if it means a non-uniform day, a chance to take part in a bake sale or to organise a sponsored activity. Sometimes there is a risk of the activities taking over from the cause, and students can lose sight of why they are fundraising — here's how to keep students involved.

One way to tackle this is to choose a school charity that your staff and students know, understand and are passionate about. This way, students will know what the charity's core purpose is, and as a result where their money is going and what it could achieve.

Start by introducing the idea in assembly to give students some thinking time. Then ask each form to nominate a charity. This could be run as a mini election within each form room where students present their chosen charity and the form group vote for a favourite.

Each form group should then have the opportunity to present their chosen charity to the rest of the year group via assembly, video recording or similar. As before, each student in that year group should then vote for their favourite, thus selecting a year group charity.

Lastly, there should be an opportunity for each of the year group's chosen charities to be presented in a more detailed way, via assembly, leaflets, posters and stalls at break and lunchtime, before the final whole-school vote. This ensures you have a charity that has been democratically elected and that all students understand. Continue to communicate the work of this charity and consider having a display board in a central area, highlighting key work and monies raised. See **Idea 20** for more ideas.

Teaching tip

If you don't want to limit yourselves to one charity, have one for each year group or key stage (you can omit the whole-school vote). Do what fits best for your setting.

IDEA 20

Purposeful fundraising

'Our students know what they are doing and why they are doing it.'

The purpose behind exciting fundraising activities can sometimes be lost on students, who might understand that their pound for non-uniform day is going to charity, but not much past that.

From a PD perspective, fundraising can develop students' empathy, but if it's a one-off activity with no thinking behind it, it is unlikely to have a long-lasting impact on a student's character.

Nominate a school charity (see **Idea 19**) and, before the fundraising event, inform students about the charity and its aims. Use terminology such as 'your pound will directly help...', so students are clear where their money is going and why.

Be specific about what different amounts of money will achieve. This information is available on most charity websites, and helps students to visualise where their money will go. It is also great if you might struggle to raise large amounts of money, as it shows that every pound does make a difference.

Educate students about why the charity exists and how it develops to meet needs, e.g. the RSPCA needed to rehome thousands of unwanted pets that were bought during the pandemic. This will help students to understand the constant need for fundraising. Also, consider fundraising for small, grassroots charities. This can seem more personal for students and someone from the charity will likely be able to come and visit your students.

When you send the money, write a letter to explain the students' PD purpose behind it. Many charities will reply, giving you something purposeful to share with students.

> **Bonus idea** ★
>
> Have a central display board that celebrates what money raised has achieved. Be literal with this: e.g. 'In term 1 we raised enough money to buy X amount of Y'.

IDEA 21

Food bank

'Our school has become a hugely valuable resource for our local community.'

Decreases in welfare, increases in the cost of living and unexpected unemployment have led to a rise in the need for food banks. This idea explores how your school could support your school or local community by setting up a food bank or mini food hub.

Different schools have different demographics, so the type of food bank you decide to offer will vary greatly.

Create a food bank: If you have high levels of poverty within your school community, you may wish to create a small, non-perishable food bank on site. To do this you will need an allocated storage space that can be locked and provide a simple drop-off point for staff (perhaps in the main reception). Make links with local supermarkets, as well as local businesses – you might gain their support as a part of their corporate social responsibility programme. Your staff might be willing to make occasional donations too. With this option, small food packages could also be sent home with students.

Create a mini food hub: Make direct links to a local food bank. Have a clear central drop-off point in school and ask for non-perishable items. You could agree a weekly or monthly collection with the food bank; if not a member of staff will need to take responsibility for this, perhaps on a rota system. The food hub could be advertised amongst your school community so that families and staff could donate.

Teaching tip

Consider the student leadership roles that could be created as a result of this idea, such as stock control where students carry out weekly stock takes and rotate products based on best before dates, or marketing where students make posters or write blogs to advertise the service.

IDEA 22

Awareness stalls

'The canteen now has a real buzz; it's great to see our students showing initiative.'

A strong PD programme should aim to get students involved in the world and to be responsible and informed citizens. Try student-led awareness stalls, allowing your students to educate and engage their peers about the issues that matter to them.

Within your student body, you will have students who are passionate about the environment, animal welfare, supporting the homeless and much more. It won't always be possible to fit all of these topics into your assembly programme, but they could be explored via awareness stalls, with a different stall taking centre stage each month or half term.

For the stall, use a central place where you can easily fit a couple of tables in a row. Ideally, this would be in a communal space students can go during lunchtime. Use the same area each time.

Be clear about your rationale and ensure this is understood by students. The stall should aim to spread awareness about an issue that the stall holders are passionate about and provide information about where students can find out more or get involved themselves.

Have a clear sign-up process to ensure all students have the opportunity to hold a stall. Give a deadline for students to submit stall proposals so that staff can check that the stall is age-appropriate and factually correct. Encourage stall holders to create something that other students can engage with, such as a leaflet, a QR code linking to further information or even a petition to sign. If your budget allows, purchase a tabletop display board that stall holders can decorate to make their stall visually appealing.

Taking it further

If this idea is popular, you may wish to have a week each half term where you host multiple stalls at once, creating a social awareness fair for students to engage with.

IDEA 23

Community gratitude

'Taking the time to stop and say thanks can mean the world.'

Schools can be the heart of the local community: a place everyone knows and where many people have links or memories.

> **Taking it further**
>
> You may wish to post more general cards through the doors of the neighbours that live in close proximity to your school, such as a summer card that reads 'staff and students from [name of school] wish you a great summer'.

There are many people and organisations within the local community who are important to us, e.g. local shopkeepers, bus drivers and school crossing patrol officers. These are often the people who see our students every day, so expressing thanks is a lovely way to bring the community together and teach students the importance of gratitude.

Ask form groups to collate names of local people and organisations that serve them in some way, e.g. the owners of the local shop near to school. Compile these to make a core 'gratitude list'. Whilst form groups are doing this, ensure their tutors are encouraging them to discuss how and why these people play an important role for staff and students.

Run a competition to design a thank-you postcard. You may wish to set certain criteria, for example that the design must incorporate the school logo. Vote for the favourite (or top three) and print enough to hand out to each of the people or organisations from the gratitude list.

Decide what message you are going to write on each postcard, ensuring this is personal to the recipient. Your student leadership group could oversee this or you could give each year group different postcards to complete.

Think carefully about how you distribute the postcards, ensuring safeguarding procedures are followed. Ideally, it would be great to have a small number of students go out to hand deliver the postcards, but if this isn't possible, post them.

IDEA 24

Little Free Library

'The students are so proud of what they've created.'

Many of you will have seen a Little Free Library in your community. The project was initially started by a man in the USA as a tribute to his mother, who was a teacher. The libraries are wooden houses that have been brightly decorated and waterproofed, ready for residents to donate and swap books.

This could be a lovely project for your students to oversee with support from staff. It gives them something tangible to produce, gives something back to the community and encourages a love of reading.

There are lots of articles online about how to design, create and manage a Little Free Library – do some research to decide on the best route for you. Have a look at littlefreelibrary.org as a starting point.

You might want to place a Little Free Library within your community, but to do this you will need to seek permission and also consider the library's upkeep, as it may be a little further away. A simpler option may be to place one on your school property, but in a place that is easily accessible, such as attached to your school gates.

Make the project a whole-school affair by involving students in the build and design of the library. This might be something your technology department or site staff could support with.

Share the upkeep. The library will need occasional retouching, waterproofing and re-painting, so form groups could take it in turn to carry out basic maintenance work.

> **Bonus idea** ★
>
> Include a motivational PD message inside the cover of each book, which could be handwritten onto sticky notes by your students e.g. 'happiness is an inside job' or 'today a reader, tomorrow a leader'.

IDEA 25

Community computing

'I was a bit worried about helping older people, but I love it!'

If there's one thing teenagers know, it's the internet! Meanwhile, some elderly people can find it difficult to learn how to navigate online platforms. Bringing the two together, by students teaching elderly citizens, not only supports your local community, but also develops their empathy and leadership skills.

Read AgeUK's information about their 'Silver Surfers' project. What they achieve in community libraries is what you could replicate in schools (at a level that suits you).

This idea will need staff support, from both a logistical and safeguarding point of view, so put a staff lead in place for this.

Identify a group of students whom you can train to run the community computing course. They will need ICT skills, as well as great communication skills, patience and empathy. Work on a ratio of 1:1, with an additional student for every three residents to cover absences. It's best to start small.

Work with the students to create a 5-week plan, keeping the outcomes realistic, e.g. setting up an email account or video call. Your ICT lead may be able to support this.

Advertising the community ICT class needs to be manageable and simple. Reach out to local community centres, community Facebook groups and libraries to tap into their existing links. You could set up a specific email to keep communications under control. This stage will need heavy staff input due to the safeguarding issues of students contacting strangers.

Your students may feel shy to begin with; you could add more staff to the first couple of sessions or practise the sessions in advance.

Taking it further

Find out where your nearest care home is and make links to see if there are any further ways that you can support elderly residents within your community.

IDEA 26

Primary helpers

'Visiting my primary buddy is the best part of my week!'

A great way to give back to the community, support younger children and develop confidence amongst your students is to work with a feeder primary school to create a buddy system.

The premise of this idea is simple: organise a time each week, half term or term for your secondary-age students to visit primary-age pupils to offer PD support, whilst also developing their own.

Make contact with the PD lead at your feeder primary school and chat with them about what their pupils might need support with. This could be help with reading, specific lesson support or simply an extra pairs of hands at breaktime.

Geography is going to massively impact the logistics of this activity. If you have a school within walking distance, it will be much easier to have regular contact. Think about this carefully and set a manageable schedule.

Likewise, think about how this will work in terms of your students' time. Ideally, you want to minimise lesson disruption, so consider either changing the contact day each time or having different groups of students visiting the primary school on rotation.

You could also work with your local primary school to set up a peer mentoring scheme (see **Ideas 11** and **12**) to support primary-age children with their behaviour or self-esteem.

Taking it further

Think about how your students could use their language skills to support English as an additional language (EAL) or new to English (NTE) students who have recently started primary school. Our multilingual students should use and celebrate all their languages, and by doing so in this way, they are also supporting the wellbeing of others.

IDEA 27

Community club

'Our students have made a positive impact in their local community.'

Teaching students about civic responsibility is an important part of a PD programme. If you set up a community volunteering club, students can play an active role in supporting and positively impacting their local community, whilst gaining valuable volunteering skills.

Community clubs are a chance for students to engage with local councils, neighbourhood groups and charities, and do something practical to make a positive difference in their community.

Work with the community club to create an action plan, focusing on the things within their area that they wish to change. This could be encouraging more wildlife through planting wildflowers, researching and presenting congestion concerns to your local council, or organising a litter pick. You could decide to have one large group, working through lots of activities. Or you could create lots of smaller clubs, each focusing on a different area.

Research what community groups already exist and contact them. Invite them to your school, or arrange an online meeting to gauge whether your community club could help them with their local missions.

Ensure you inform your local councillors. They are often very keen to liaise with schools and will be able to give lots of advice about other local projects your students could take part in.

When advertising to students, make it clear that they will be working hard and getting their hands dirty! There will also be a time commitment, meaning that students will sometimes need to stay after school.

> **Bonus idea** ★
>
> Order community club hoodies for students to wear on the days when they are out in the community. This will ensure they are comfortable while raising awareness of your club and what it is trying to achieve.

Part 4

Careers education

IDEA 28

Real models vs role models

'Finally, I feel like I can see "me".'

Whilst it's important to explore the contributions of role models, it's also vital to open teenagers' eyes to real models, individuals making a difference and doing great things in their communities.

Teaching tip

Share your real models with your students too – tell them about the people who had a positive impact on your life, your education or within your local area.

Ensuring young people have a variety of role models to look up to is a worthwhile thing to do. Sharing the stories of famous people who have made a global impact can be hugely inspiring. However, for many young people, these role models can feel detached from their reality due to the monumental things the role models have achieved. It's worth sharing examples of people they know in real life alongside famous icons.

Look amongst your staff body. Would anyone who has overcome personal or academic challenges be willing to share their story during an assembly, e.g. a staff member who had to retake GCSEs or who came to the UK as an immigrant?

Among your alumni, think about those who have success stories that will resonate with your current students, e.g. the student who arrived at school not speaking a word of English who went on to study literature at sixth form, or the student with a poor attendance record who is doing well in their apprenticeship. Keep in touch and invite them back – the power of a peer sharing their story is huge.

Consider the great things that are happening in your local community and the people who are driving these projects, e.g. somebody who started a community foodbank, runs a youth project or is involved in fundraising for local facilities. Share their stories with your students.

IDEA 29

Flat pack team building hack

'Building the steps took a while, but we all felt proud once it was done!'

Careers education isn't just about jobs, it's a way of providing opportunities for students to develop their communication skills and ability to work as a team. This is a hands-on, fun activity that students love.

Find a basic, self-assembly wooden step and buy one per group of students. The idea is that each group will come up with a specific purpose for the step and then build, decorate and market it, before finally presenting their finished product.

Organise students into groups of five or six. Explain that they will be taking a basic wooden step and repurposing it to suit a target market, e.g. decorating it to be suitable for a child's bedroom or turning it into a shelf for potted plants. Encourage them to use their imagination and think creatively. They will then need to work together to build their steps, and then create their vision using the materials provided to them. They will also need to work on their pitch and practise presenting this as a group.

- Get into groups.
- Come up with a design concept and product name.
- Build the steps.
- Decorate or repurpose the steps.
- Create a pitch.
- Practise the pitch.

Taking it further

If your school plans dropdown days, where students come off timetable to take part in PD activities, this challenge could work well. This way, students could spend the full day immersed in this activity and get really creative.

IDEA 30

My life at 30

'It's lovely to hear students talk about the type of future they want for themselves as adults.'

Students often get to discuss the job they want in the future, but adulthood is more than that — how often are students asked to consider the type of life they want for themselves as adults?

Taking it further

Have form tutors keep hold of these posters as a tool to stimulate pastoral discussions in the future.

A core aspect of careers education is ensuring that students have the information and guidance needed to make choices about their future. Students might be well-versed in talking about the career they want but may not have had the opportunity to consider where, how and why this links to the type of life they dream of having when they are adults.

Gather large sheets of paper, glue, coloured pens and a wide variety of pictures, such as of money, houses, travel, family, university, clothing, hobbies, etc. At the start of the activity, ask students to close their eyes and imagine being 30. Encourage them to silently consider what they might look like, where they might live, who they might live with, what their job might be, etc. Allow some time for students to discuss their initial thoughts with their peers. If students are confident, allow for some feedback.

Allow students the freedom to create their own 'My Life at 30' posters. Encourage purposeful discussions, e.g. 'What type of salary might be needed to fund this lifestyle and what is therefore needed from you?', 'Do you agree with the idea of "work hard, play hard"?' or 'Do you see more value in income or in job satisfaction?'. Students are not expected to know all the answers, but this gets them to see their future careers as something that will hugely impact their way of life as adults.

IDEA 31

Careers in the curriculum

'I love my subject, and it's been great to share the different career paths that it can lead to with my students.'

Careers education shouldn't be a standalone event that happens during National Careers Week or via careers interview. Use some of your curriculum time to introduce students to the careers that link to each subject area. Who better to inspire them about subject specific careers than the curriculum experts themselves?

Students can struggle to make links between the subjects they love and what these could lead to. Strategically bringing careers into the curriculum can support this, and allows subject teachers to share their passion differently.

Communicate with subject leaders to agree on a whole-school approach and ensure expectations are clear. It's important teachers are involved as they may have concerns about curriculum time or additional planning.

Keep it manageable. Pick 2–3 weeks in the year to devote to careers in the curriculum. Be flexible in your approach – ensure all classes in all subjects get careers input, but allow subject leads to decide on the amount of time to commit, e.g. a 10-minute starter or full lesson.

Keep it simple. Sessions could involve staff sharing with students their post-16 options and reasons for choosing them or planning a starter that introduces students to an unusual career within that subject.

Teachers could share information with students about further and higher education courses for their subject, both nearby and further afield.

Subjects could pick an element of their curriculum and then discuss careers that link to it, such as natural disasters in geography and careers such as volcanology or seismology.

> **Taking it further**
>
> Reach out to local universities, businesses, and organisations. As a part of their corporate responsibility strategy they might be willing to come to speak at your school.

IDEA 32

Future learning

'I used to have a very fixed idea about what my education path should be, but now I can see it doesn't have to be that way.'

Students can have fixed ideas about their future education path. This could be due to a lack of understanding or family influence.

Teaching tip

As a piece of careers homework, identify a range of careers and ask students to research the different routes that lead to them.

Students might think that the only education available past 18 is university, and that this means moving away from home and committing to tuition fees. Or they might believe that university is not for them; that it is beyond their reach. This can turn some students off and stop them from exploring future learning routes. Consider rephrasing how you communicate with students, using the term 'future learning' rather than solely referring to one option.

Students need to know that future learning isn't always linear, and it doesn't look the same for everyone. They need to be supported in seeing the bigger picture and the range of routes available. Yes, some students will pass all their GCSEs at level 2, go on to study A levels and then move away to university. Yes, some students will start working and earning money straight away. Both options, and others, are OK.

Start conversations about Levels 1–6 early on, and make it clear that progression through education levels can be non-linear. Students should see progression through the levels as something positive to support and further develop their future learning, not as a competition with their peers.

Don't limit information to Year 11. If you've planned an assembly about apprenticeships or university, allow all students to attend. If you have external further or higher education visitors coming into your school, arrange it so KS3 gets some input. Share open day information with the wider school body. There's nothing stopping younger students going – get them interested in their future learning as soon as possible.

When looking at moving up through Levels 4, 5, 6 and beyond, ensure students know there are academic, vocational and work routes to all of these. They also need to know there isn't an upper age limit to this progression. They might get to Level 3, work for a while, and then decide to progress further through the levels.

Ensure students know what their future learning might look like if they don't quite get the grades needed in Year 11. They need to see that they haven't failed, just that their pathway will look a little different. Advertise and educate about Level 1 and 2 courses as well as any 'step up to A Level' type courses that your local further education provisions offer. Students need to be aware of these so they don't lose sight of their future learning aspirations.

Modern apprenticeships are worlds away from what they were 10 years ago. Educate students about them from KS3 so that they're a genuine option when students begin making post-16 choices in KS4. Ensure you educate parents too, as there may be a lack of understanding or prejudice around apprenticeships, which means students might feel pressure from their families to go down the traditional academic route. Invite apprenticeship providers to KS4 parent evenings or create an information sheet to be sent home.

When teaching students about university, explore all options and don't presume all will want to go straight from college or sixth form and move away. The cost of living and personal family relationships means that, for many, moving away is not an option, so also explore what your local area has to offer. Make them aware of online options such as Open University as well as part-time study routes. Introduce them to the concept of mature students too – learning never has to stop!

> **Bonus idea** ★
>
> If staff are happy to share, create a future learning display board that highlights and celebrates the different learning routes that staff have taken.

IDEA 33

Developing professional relationships

'Taking time to look outwards and get to grips with who and what is available in my local area was hugely worthwhile.'

School is fast-paced and there never seems to be enough hours in the day, but spending time making links with local post-16 providers, charities, businesses and organisations will save you time in the future and add a richness to your PD programme.

Having a bank of people who know you, know your school and are happy to make links is invaluable. Remember, corporate social responsibility is a big thing for organisations too, so reach out to them!

Find out when your local further and higher education open days are and attend them. Search out the people responsible for school liaison, chat with the faculty leads, and get as many contacts as you can. Having that initial face-to-face contact will make future conversations more personalised and will hopefully lead to lots of opportunities for school visits.

Search for local charities and make links with these (the Neighbourly website is a great starting point). If students support these charities, this is great for their PD and the charities benefit too. Charity staff may also work with your students to explain the charity sector or the benefits of volunteering.

Write to local businesses telling them about your school's demographic and ask for a meeting to discuss potential collaborations. Many sector areas are underrepresented by certain groups, so be savvy about this, e.g. by contacting local STEM organisations about working with a group of girls at your school.

Taking it further

Reach out to your parent community, explaining your vision and the desire to make links with local employers. This is something primary schools utilise quite well but can be an opportunity that is missed at secondary.

IDEA 34

Sector experience days

'I didn't just get to experience one job, I experienced a sector.'

Work experience is a key feature of the Gatsby Benchmarks, which schools use to self-report their careers education progress. Planning both simulated and immersive activities that allow students to experience a whole sector can be hugely motivating for them.

A traditional work experience model can be great, but can also lack aspiration and variety due to age and training limits. A student wanting to become a lawyer is not going to help out with a court case during work experience! Divide your cohort (this may be a full-year group) into groups of 20 to 30 students to make external visits manageable. The number of groups is the number of sector packages needed.

Find out the popular sectors among your students and try to include these in your sector packages. If this isn't possible, choose a range of sectors to offer variety e.g. computing, public services or creative industries.

Consider how many days you will provide: you could start small with one day per sector or put on a full week of activities. Ask organisations to send someone to speak to your students, run workshops or even a simulated activity related to their roles. Be guided by your capacity and the existing links you have.

Reach out to local universities – the experience could include a taster day to help students learn about higher education. For health sector days, make links with ambulance services who offer training to young people, as well as Medical Mavericks who provide workshops to simulate medical procedures. Large chain hotels may offer tours to students, allowing them to see a range of careers relating to travel and tourism.

Teaching Tip

What you can provide will depend on your location and the links you have established, which is another reason to invest time in reaching out to local universities and businesses.

IDEA 35

I'll tell you what I want...

'Involving our students in creating our careers provision was the best thing we ever did.'

Your school's career provision exists to ensure your students are provided with opportunities and education to broaden their horizons, increase their aspirations, and ensure they understand their next steps. It's all about them.

> **Taking it further**
>
> East Learning provides ready-to-go, online surveys to complete with your students. This includes a CEIAG survey, which will provide you with lots of personalised information to support your provision.

Your careers provision, although guided by the Gatsby Benchmarks, does not have to fit a certain model. Unlike a GCSE subject where a specification has to be followed and where all students take the same exam, your provision should be personalised to the needs and wants of your cohort – and how will you know what these are if you don't ask?

Each year during form time, carry out online career surveys. These will provide you with data regarding university or apprenticeship interest, the number of students who have a clear idea of their next steps, or the sectors that are currently the most popular. You can then use this information to guide your provision and prioritise interventions.

Hold termly focus groups with key cohorts of students to gather qualitative information. This should include students who are demonstrating behavioural habits that could indicate a future risk of not being in education, employment or training (NEET), such as low attendance. These focus groups can be informal, and led by a teacher, form tutor or pastoral lead. The key is to find out information that can help drive your initiatives, e.g. if students are saying they don't want to go to college because they want to earn money, do more to teach about apprenticeships.

IDEA 36

Breaking stereotypes

'We want students to know that they aren't limited by their identity.'

Careers education is as much about raising aspirations as it is about specific careers or qualifications. For students to be truly aspirational, they mustn't feel like certain careers are beyond their reach because of their gender, race or any other aspect of their identity.

There are masses of stereotypes about careers. Many students will sadly presume they are incapable of certain careers because they can't see themselves in those roles.

Think about what your students see. Carry out some quality assurance with your subject leads to consider the images they use in their slides. Are images racially diverse? Do they show all genders in positions of power? Looking at resources through fresh eyes can make stereotypes that you weren't even aware of stand out.

Explore career stereotypes within your PSHE lessons. Carry out activities such as matching the image of a person to the career, or listing jobs they associate with men or women, and then unpick this. Allow time to explore the origins of these stereotypes and offer alternatives.

Introduce students to real models (see **Idea 28**) who have been successful in a range of careers, and allow them to see themselves by ensuring you show them a range of different identities. Keeping in touch with ex-students via an alumni scheme will hugely support this. Nothing will help to inspire students quicker than introducing an ex-student (whom current students can identify with) who has gone on to be happy and successful in their chosen career.

Taking it further

Carry out extensive work in this area before students choose their KS4 options. For example, ensure boys know the different careers that could come out of a health and social care course that could suit their future aspirations, likewise with girls and PE.

IDEA 37

LMI, why?

'Knowing more about the careers available where I live has helped me to make decisions about my future learning.'

Being aware of Labour Market Information (LMI), such as the industries that are experiencing the most growth and the largest employers in a specific region, can help students make informed decisions about the options and the careers they choose.

Understanding LMI is especially powerful when considering the impact it can have on social mobility; encouraging students to research and consider readily available careers, pay progression, and opportunities for promotion. Build computing time into your PSHE lessons, or set research as homework so that students can get to grips with LMI at a personal level.

Build personal reflection into your PSHE or form time programme. Encourage students to think about their likes and dislikes and how these link to potential careers. For example, if a student wants to become an accountant but hates maths, this might need to be unpicked. Use the National Careers Services online skills assessment to help students make links.

Indeed is another great website for students to explore in PSHE. It has lots of articles that explore salaries, working abroad and growing industries. It also includes reviews for lots of well-known companies – a great tool for discussing job satisfaction with your students.

Prospects also has a skills assessment that students could use in PSHE when teaching about degrees and Level 4+ qualifications. The online function allows students to type in a degree and find all the careers that link to this qualification. Students could then search online to see whether these jobs exist locally – a great LMI investigation.

> **Bonus idea** ★
>
> When something new comes to your local area, such as a new restaurant, transport system or care home, encourage form tutors to discuss the careers that will become available as a result.

IDEA 38

The early signs – NEET

'It's never too early to start career intervention work.'

There are huge complexities that surround students becoming NEET; if we begin to tackle these in KS4, it can often be too late. Be proactive in identifying students at risk and provide them with additional, personalised career support.

Involve the careers team in the Year 6 transition to work alongside the SEND, pastoral and safeguarding teams as they process information about students who could be vulnerable. Each term, add pre-NEET to your middle leadership team meeting agenda and ask staff to identify students who are consistently disengaged with learning across subjects and may need intervention.

Start with light touch intervention in Year 7. Hold half-termly 'hot chocolate mornings' where a group of identified students can have breakfast with the careers lead and discuss their likes and dislikes. This allows gentle talk about the future and for the career lead to develop a bond with these students. Continue these meetings termly across Years 8 and 9.

When the cohort reach Year 9, schedule a few small visits to local post-16 providers and get the students excited about the possibility of attending college or sixth form. Towards the end of Year 9, ensure they have time in a smaller group to find out more and ask questions to apprenticeship providers. This could be after an apprenticeship assembly.

Ramp things up in Years 10 and 11. At this point, the group of identified students should have regular check-ins and one-to-one career interviews with the careers lead at key points, such as after mock exam results, a college interview or a period of low attendance.

Taking it further

Involve parents as much as possible, from as early as possible, in a supportive, non-threatening way. Celebrate the student's successes and keep the parents informed.

Mental health and wellbeing

Part 5

IDEA 39

Wellbeing pack

'Receiving this package from school was great, it made me feel supported and well cared for.'

When our students leave us, it can feel as though we are sending them out into the abyss. This idea ensures they have sufficient signposting to see them through the weeks and months ahead.

Creating a wellbeing pack (physical or online) ensures students have age-appropriate contact details and places they can go if they need support. Think about what you have shared already. Remind them those places exist separately from school and that they can still access them as school leavers.

Include a range of young people-friendly sexual health clinics that they can access. It's vital students know where these places are and how to get to them, so consider providing further information (e.g. 'behind Nando's in the centre of town') – it needs to feel accessible.

The pack should also include specific support for your LGBTQ+ students. If you work in a school, contact your feeder sixth forms and colleges to find out if they have an LGBTQ+ group, and include this information.

Outline how and when students can access career information and guidance in the months after they leave school and ensure they know how to contact the careers manager. Leaving school doesn't mean their careers support and guidance ceases to exist.

Many students may wish to use the summer to work or volunteer. Ensure the wellbeing pack provides contact details of reputable volunteer organisations, information regarding their rights in the workplace and where they can access citizen support.

Taking it further

Contact local FE and HE providers to see if they can contribute. This will help to bridge the transition between the two.

IDEA 40

What's behind the door?

'How much time do students spend sitting on the loo, looking ahead? Might as well give them something positive to look at!'

As much as we want students to come to us directly, they might not always be ready. Toilet signs can help to signpost students to a wide range of topics affecting their lives.

Consider buying clip frames to fix directly onto the door frame – posters will easily become damaged if not protected. Use these frames to display posters with key information, and make the most of public health campaigns created specifically for this age group.

Ensure the information is personalised to the needs of your cohort, and liaise with the safeguarding and pastoral teams so that the information displayed is what your students need. For example, if there is an increase in reports of sexual harassment, your door signs might include information about misogyny, how to be an ally or how to report it.

If you have separate toilets for boys and girls, tailor the information accordingly and think about your target audience, e.g. by displaying campaigns that break down male mental health stigma in your boys' toilets. If you do not have gender-neutral facilities, ensure your posters contain some gender-neutral language so as not to alienate any students who may be trans or non-binary.

Align the information to what is being explored within the PSHE curriculum – being able to see signposting information that relates to this could be hugely useful. Use key points in the year to display key information, e.g. bereavement support around Mother's/Father's Day and advice about healthy relationships and consent near Valentine's Day.

Taking it further

Gather feedback from your students to directly inform what you display.

IDEA 41

Student health and wellbeing charter

'We have worked together to create a charter that will help us all to be physically and emotionally healthy.'

A student health and wellbeing charter outlines the concrete actions at your school that place young people's health and wellbeing at the very centre of your ethos.

Teaching tip

Use form time to support discussion, with students critically evaluating each statement to make reference to their health and wellbeing.

The charter should be student-led, publicly displayed, and valued by your whole school community. Consult your whole student body about what they require from school to be emotionally and physically healthy. Your role is to support and facilitate, not to take over.

- Use online forms to collate initial ideas. Once you've received feedback, group these into areas, e.g. diet, relationships. Consider a range of 'the school will' and 'we will' statements for each group. For example, 'the school will set realistic homework deadlines' and 'we will communicate with our teachers if we can't meet a deadline'.
- Next, check your students are happy with the 'we will' statements and school leaders are confident that the 'school will' statements are achievable. You don't want to publish something that cannot be achieved!
- Once the charter is finalised, make it look appealing. If you have a marketing team or computing whizz within your school community, use them! You can then celebrate the charter, share it with all stakeholders and display it around school and on your website.
- Be sure to refer to it regularly and review it in line with your policy review procedures, ensuring the charter remains front and centre and is adapted when needed.

IDEA 42

Staff health and wellbeing charter

'We are teaching our students that prioritising our health and wellbeing is something we all value.'

We must lead by example. Creating a visible staff wellbeing charter shows students that staff care about their own wellbeing and each other's. It helps them to see that wellbeing is something that all of us can and should prioritise at all stages of our lives.

Consider who the staff drive team are going to be and make this a voluntary role. Ideally, your drive team should represent all of the school, e.g. the SLT, middle leaders, teaching staff, early career teachers (ECTs), administration, pastoral, safeguarding, site, etc.

Involve your union reps, as they will have a clear idea as to what the current stressors are within the workforce and can offer valuable insights. Create staff wellbeing reps to be the school 'figureheads', to whomstaff can go with ideas on how to drive the charter forward.

When planning the consultation, use time already allocated within the 1265 rule, or have it as an optional event. Keep the consultation positive (cake and coffee help!).

Start the consultation with positive discussion questions, e.g. 'What makes me feel valued at school?' or 'How do I like my work to be recognised?'. Positivity will encourage staff to be solution-focused.

Read **Idea 41** for how your staff wellbeing charter could be created. Remember to display this charter where students can see it. This idea supports students as it teaches them that wellbeing is vital for everyone and is something we should all be able to discuss and consider.

> **Taking it further**
>
> If form tutors feel comfortable, ask them to talk through the staff charter and explain why it's important. They could then ask their form to do the same with the student charter.

IDEA 43

Who does what, and so what?

'They no longer feel like people that are unapproachable. I know who they are and how they can help me.'

School leadership structures can sometimes be a confusing thing to navigate for students (and staff!). This can lead to missed opportunities because students don't know where to go for help. We have key roles for a reason, so share and celebrate these!

Start with your school website. This is simple to do and can be visually organised in a way that makes sense. This is great for staff and parents, but will students use it? Perhaps not, so what else could you do?

- Create a display board in a central area, to include headshots, job titles and brief descriptions.
- When describing roles, use language that suits young people. Write in a way they will understand and then check this before displaying it.
- Make staff roles a key feature of September 'welcome back' assemblies, and use this opportunity to remind students who the key leaders are.
- Consider how you wish your student body to communicate with school leaders and how this can be organised in a useful and time-efficient manner. Do you want this to be a completely open door? If so, do students know where the key offices are? Do you want students to use Google Classroom, Teams or school email? If so, has the etiquette been clearly explained?
- School leaders could hold regular school surgeries to encourage the student population to communicate with them freely and openly (for more information, see **Idea 72**).

Taking it further

What about school governance? Could you implement some of the ideas above to improve familiarity with the governance team?

IDEA 44

Wellbeing digital wall

'We know that teenagers and the internet go hand-in-hand, so why not make this a force for good?'

Teenagers spend a lot of their time on the internet. The online environment is a world they have grown up in; they are comfortable with it and use it with ease. Why not tap into this intrinsic aspect of teen culture and use it to ensure students have 24-hour access to online support and wellbeing services?

Schools can use apps such as Google Jamboard, Padlet, Wakelet or Lino to curate their own digital wellbeing walls that students can access whenever they need, 24 hours a day, 365 days a year.

Start with the basics: consider the well-known and trusted organisations that offer wellbeing support to young people, and ensure your digital wall contains their logos with direct links to their websites, e.g. ChildLine, the Samaritans and Kooth. This will ensure your students can go to core organisations if they require them.

What are the local services that your students might need access to and support from? For example, youth drop-ins, sexual health clinics or local libraries that offer quiet places to study. Your digital wall could signpost to local services and provide opening times and directions.

Ensure your digital wall reflects your school's safeguarding trends. You may wish to have links to specific services that can offer support in areas such as substance abuse, self-harm and domestic violence. Digital walls also allow staff to post videos and images. Use these functions to incorporate some fun and positivity into this online space. You could include workout videos, guided meditation and even your top five funniest YouTube videos.

> **Taking it further**
>
> Promote the digital wellbeing wall with students and parents and seek annual feedback to ensure the wall continues to meet the needs of your students.

IDEA 45

Ask It Basket – next generation!

'Students understand what this is, so they use it.'

The vast majority of secondary-age students will understand the purpose of the legendary 'Ask It Basket' because they used one at primary school. As young children it is likely that there was a box in their classroom where they could write down a worry or question to be answered by their teacher. It makes sense to carry over wellbeing methods that work – if students are engaging with this in primary, why get rid of it in secondary?

Ask It Baskets should remain, although they might need a reboot for an older generation.

A simple adaptation could be to change the name to something more grown-up, so ask your students what they think it should be called. Have a whole-school vote to decide on the final name.

Ask your site team to install a couple of 'letterboxes' in central, yet tucked-away, locations. Make this a whole-school affair by asking your technology department to support with their creation. You could even have a school competition to choose the design to be painted onto the letterboxes.

Form tutors may wish to design a shoe box with their form, and keep their own basket in their base room. Some students may feel more comfortable engaging with a basket that is kept within their form room, especially as this closely mimics primary.

Taking it further

Consider an online version. Set up an email address with the same or a similar name to your physical letterbox. This gives students another option to 'ask it' and will encourage more students to reach out.

IDEA 46

KS4 and KS5 transition

'I felt really worried about starting my GCSEs, but luckily my teachers were there to help me with this transition.'

Year 6 to 7 transition is huge – the residentials, special assemblies and transition days. We do it because we know it is significant to our young people. This idea expands to KS3 and KS4 too.

Transition at other key points is just as important, such as KS3 to KS4, or from KS4 to KS5. We may view these as less emotionally demanding, because students are older or because they may not be leaving our setting, but these are still huge transitions that can impact students' wellbeing. As a staff body we need to acknowledge that these transitions are important and provide outlets for our students to come to us if needed.

Ensure there is a dedicated assembly at each transition point that focuses on the *wellbeing* aspect of transition, such as how choosing options might feel stressful and how to deal with this stress by talking with trusted adults, and not rushing decisions.

At each transition point, have at least one dedicated form time session that is discussion-based. Consider creating conversation cards that students can use to prompt discussion about their feelings towards transition.

Ensure that wellbeing is included on the discussion notes for parents' evenings that take place during key transition points, and provide parents with websites that can offer advice on how to support their child.

Work with subject leaders to ensure that workload and resilience are on the curriculum map for the first few lessons of KS4 courses to ensure they are discussed.

Taking it further

If possible, ask students (past and present) who have been through this transition to speak to their peers who are currently experiencing it.

IDEA 47

Being mindful of mindfulness

'All of us can benefit from pausing to focus on the present.'

Modern teenage life can be fast-paced. Students are growing up in the social media era where they are bombarded with constant online notifications and visuals. Use PD time at school to counteract this by explicitly teaching mindfulness.

Taking it further

Use PSHE lessons as your guinea pig, then work out what's popular and look to incorporate these so they become whole-school practice.

Being mindful, and knowing how to switch off and truly relax isn't something teenagers necessarily know how to do. Being relaxed can be confused with being bored. Students might struggle to find a method of mindfulness which they enjoy and doesn't involve a screen.

Incorporate traditional mindfulness activities into your PD programme as it's unlikely this is something students will learn to do independently. This allows staff to model activities such as basic meditation and deep breathing. But, don't sell this as the only way to relax – it isn't for everyone.

Allow opportunities for students to consider how they feel in the moment, such as when they are receiving praise, or about to go into an exam. This encourages students to be more aware of their emotions.

Incorporate grounding exercises into high-stress points within the school calendar, e.g. pause before an assessment to encourage students to be aware of their senses. Use the 'think of five things you can see, four things you can hear, etc.' method.

Incorporate a simple stretch activity into the start of your PSHE lessons. Acknowledge that teenagers get tired and might struggle to be seated for long periods. Guide them through a couple of seated stretches and encourage them to think about how it makes their body feel.

IDEA 48

Friendship club

'We recognise that some of our students struggle during social times, so we did something about it.'

Navigating friendship groups, dealing with noisy canteens and transitioning to a different way to 'play' is extra-challenging for some young people as they move up to secondary school.

Offering a friendship club as a part of your extracurricular offer can help these students feel safe and comfortable, whilst also giving a chance to implicitly teach social skills.

Think carefully about where the club will be based and who will run it. Ideally, choose a room close to the canteen area so that students aren't completely shut off, to support reintegration. Ensure the person overseeing this club is familiar with pastoral approaches to support students who struggle socially.

Consider how you launch this club – you are providing a unique offer for the particular students who might need it, so a big whole-school launch is likely to be unsuitable. Work with your wider pastoral teams and form tutors to ensure students are made aware, or use the backs of doors to advertise (**Idea 40**).

Ask students what they want from this club – they may just want a place to hang out, play games, draw, etc. Slowly build in self-esteem activities e.g. 'Fill your plate' or 'A-Z of awesomeness' (see the online resources). Keep activities fun and relaxed. Over time, gently encourage students to go into the main school social spaces. Ensure they know the friendship club base is still there if they need you, but encourage snippets of reintegration into the full school body, e.g. 'It's sunny, why don't we finish up 10 minutes early and you go out for some fresh air?'.

> **Taking it further**
>
> If students agree, consider some peer-led coaching sessions to run during this time (see **Idea 12**).

Part 6

Form time and assembly

IDEA 49

Why?

'We must take every opportunity to explore the bigger picture with our students.'

Most of us will have a reason for working with young people; this is our 'why', and it can keep us going when the job gets tough. This idea encourages students to consider their 'why', so they can keep this is mind when faced with their own challenges.

Taking it further

This is also a lovely activity to run with staff during INSET days, as it can create a positive start to the year.

Sharing your 'why' and supporting students to consider their own 'why' is a fantastic project to undertake via your assembly and form time programme.

Think carefully about who is going to lead your 'why' assembly. Ideally, you want to use two or three staff members (don't have staff members who are too similar, diversity works well for this) who can communicate positively with students and don't mind opening up about their lives.

Each staff member who is leading the assembly should create a slide that highlights their personal 'why' – if they are happy to, students love to see photos! The slide might include things like their parents (wanting to make them proud), a previous teacher (who inspired them), passion for their subject, etc. These slides will form the basis of the assembly.

As students enter the assembly hall, the screen should simply display the word 'why'. The staff delivering will then talk through their 'why' – they must emphasise that, on difficult days, they think back to their 'why' and this gives them the motivation they need to be resilient. This is also powerful as it tells students that adults also have bad days where they need to dig deep.

Once the staff have presented their 'why', they should invite students to think about what their 'why' is in terms of being successful at school, and why this is important to them. If appropriate, ask some students to volunteer their initial thoughts.

Following this assembly, further independent work should be completed during form time (or PSHE). This should begin with the form tutor talking through their 'why' with their form group, allowing students to hear from their 'key person'.

Students should then be given time to mind-map their own 'why'. Allow time for students to discuss this with each other and their tutor. Students should then aim to condense their mind map into a sentence (or two). The form tutor should model this so students can see the process in action. The final sentence might read something like 'I want to do well at school so that I can get the grades I need to become a lawyer. I also want to make my family and myself proud'.

Once students have written their 'why' sentences, they need to be stored somewhere that is easy to access. If you use planners, students can write the 'why' sentences in there, or add them as a note next to the student's name in Arbor, Classcharts or similar. If you have a form board, you may also wish to create a display board.

Their 'whys' should be referred to frequently. They should be a positive reference for staff when having pastoral conversations with students, allowing for a productive conversation that keeps future goals in mind. They can also be shared with the school careers staff to act as a starting point for career interviews.

> **Bonus idea** ★
>
> If you have a Year 11 leavers' assembly, collate students' 'whys' and give them these to look back on. This is a lovely reflection activity that students thoroughly enjoy.

IDEA 50

Assembly calendar

'I loved seeing my identity being celebrated, it made me feel seen.'

Assemblies are a time when your school community comes together to achieve a common purpose, be that to celebrate, learn or reflect. Work together to create an assembly calendar that celebrates your community and reflects on key dates.

Working collaboratively will ensure that key dates are given time for reflection and multiple cultures are celebrated, giving chances for shared celebration of cultural capital.

Start by listing the overall themes your calendar should include, e.g. religious observance, safeguarding campaigns, national awareness campaigns and key school dates. Send this out to form groups so that staff and students can collaborate and come up with additional ideas. This stage is very important, as to be truly celebratory, the calendar should incorporate the collective values of your whole community.

Discuss with safeguarding leads. There are many public health campaigns and safety awareness initiatives out there. Your designated safeguarding lead (DSL) will be able to inform you which are the most beneficial for your cohort.

Look at the cultural demographic of your students and ensure all groups can share their ideas. Pay close attention to minority groups to ensure their culture is celebrated, e.g. if you have Romanian students in your school, consider an assembly to mark Great Union Day.

Once you have your calendar mapped, think about delivery and open this out to everyone! Some of the most powerful assemblies are the ones that are student-led with staff support. Share your calendar on the school website – it is a document to be celebrated!

Taking it further

Can you bring the assembly into break time? Consider having student-led stalls at break and lunch where students can find out more information about the assembly themes (see **Idea 22**).

Bonus idea ★

Use form time to support this further, if assembly time or space is tight – use Teams (or similar) to deliver live assemblies into form rooms Alternatively, consider using sites such as Loom to pre-record assemblies.

IDEA 51

Culture assemblies

'It's been an honour to listen to our students share their culture.'

Assemblies are a fantastic way to celebrate the different cultures and passions within your school community. Incorporate student-led assemblies into your school ethos and curriculum areas to create a culture where students sharing their cultures with others is seen as the norm and celebrated. Assemblies provide a large audience, so they are a great way to do this!

Share the vision with subject leaders. Ask them to think about work that goes on within their curriculum that celebrates cultures and diversity and work with them to fill a slot on the assembly calendar. Obvious examples include poetry in English, dance or a musical performance. This helps strengthen a diverse curriculum, provides an opportunity for students to perform, and is exciting and enjoyable for the audience.

Meet with your drama lead. KS4 classes will likely need to produce a performance for their exam piece – could it be linked to a cultural event, e.g. Black History Month? It will give students valuable practice and form an exciting feature of your assembly calendar.

Consider your extracurricular offer. Are any of the groups working on a performance or creating something that could be shared with their peers in assembly, e.g. could a debate club host a live debate?

Ensure the whole student body is invited to attend. Ask and encourage students to come to you with their ideas: this can be particularly powerful during religious observance assemblies. I once witnessed Muslim students perform the Islamic call to prayer during an Eid assembly and you could hear a pin drop.

Taking it further

Open this out to your whole staff body, and allow them the space to share something about their culture. I vividly remember an assembly led by a Peruvian teacher (in full traditional dress) on *Día de los Muertos*. You might be pleasantly surprised by what is offered.

Bonus idea ★

Whilst building student confidence, it might be that the assembly is recorded and played on a large screen, rather than being live.

IDEA 52

Who's who?

'It takes a village.'

All school staff play a role in supporting students, but do we ever publicly introduce everyone and celebrate what they do? Let students know who your school's key people are.

> **Taking it further**
>
> You could also create a 'Who's who?' display, to keep all of your teams front and centre.

You will likely have an administration team who print and prepare resources, site staff who keep the building safe and maintained, kitchen staff who cook and serve food, and many more. Hold a 'who's who' assembly to give thanks to different teams. It creates a sense of community, supports wellbeing and ensures students know all the adults within the school.

First, check that each team is happy to attend. Some might find it difficult due to their role, or some might feel too embarrassed to speak in front of many people. It needs to be on their terms. If they can't attend in person, show their photo as you talk about and celebrate their role.

Talk about the importance of community, and how everyone plays a crucial role. Discuss the staff who are well-known, e.g. teachers and pastoral leads, but then ask 'Who else ensures that our community is successful?'.

Introduce each team as a collective, saying a few words about the team members' roles and, importantly, how they have a positive impact on staff and students. Then give public personal thanks: 'On behalf of the school, thank you for all you do.'

Finish by re-emphasising respect and community, and encourage students to think about how they can respect staff, their school and themselves. This can also help to break down hierarchies that may exist in students' minds. You are showing that every person is valuable and should be respected.

IDEA 53

What do you think about that then?

'I used to feel a bit nervous about discussing current affairs in class, but this structure has given me more confidence.'

Form time lends itself well to discussing current affairs — it's a great way to get students talking, to engage in the world around them and to enhance your citizenship offer.

Discussing current affairs can be difficult, lack structure or escalate quickly. Having a well-planned, well-practised and clearly communicated format for discussing these topics is a huge support for staff. Delegate the role of creating and distributing resources with a simple template, ideally a week in advance. This gives form tutors time to familiarise themselves with the topic.

Start with topics that are engaging, but also feel safe, e.g. an environmental protest or an advance in technology. This allows time for staff and students to get used to the structure and for ground rules to be firmly embedded (see **Idea 64**). The template could include:

- Slide 1. Show an image to represent the topic. Students are to discuss what they know or what they think the topic might be.
- Slide 2. Learn about the topic, perhaps by linking to a short news clip or article.
- Slide 3. Three simple questions to discuss in groups, (Why? What? How?).
- Slide 4. Pose an agree/disagree statement, and ask students to move to a position along an imaginary line that represents their viewpoint, allowing for a brief discussion.
- Slide 5. Summary. Close the conversations, summarise both sides and thank students for their respectful discussions.

Taking it further

Each department could take it in turns to find a topic, which could be related to their subject area. An example slideshow is available in the online resources — you could circulate this (or edit it first) to give a standard structure.

IDEA 54

Form time notices

'This feels manageable and I'm confident I'm not missing key information.'

Form tutors are expected to check equipment, distribute letters and give out reminders, on top of delivering the actual form time programme. Make things simpler for them by streamlining the process for distributing key messages.

Have all messages typed directly onto a central slide deck and shown to form groups on an identified day each week. This ensures no messages are missed or communicated incorrectly, as well as reducing the number of emails a form tutor receives.

- Identify an area on your school SharePoint (or equivalent) that all staff can access.
- Create a central folder called 'Form time messages' and give everyone editing rights. This is where all your form time message slideshows will sit.
- Within this central folder, create duplicate folders, one for each half term (six in total), and label these clearly, e.g. HT1, HT2.
- Within each half term folder, create duplicate folders for each week, clearly labelled, e.g. w/c 6.11.23, w/c 13.11.23, etc.
- Create a simple slide consisting of a table with two columns, one headed 'Who?' and the other 'Message'. Copy this slide into each weekly folder.

Communicate this method to all staff – this must be advertised as the agreed way to get messages into form groups. Ensure staff identify which groups the message is for, e.g. all Year 9 boys, and include information about where students can go for additional information if needed.

Taking it further

Encourage students' independence by setting up an online classroom for form groups (e.g. Teams, Google Classroom), and attaching a view-only link to the form time message's slides. This is also a useful tool for parents to access from home if needed.

IDEA 55

Check in, check out!

'I like to know they are settled for the week ahead and then ready for the weekend.'

A form tutor is a student's go-to person; they are often the first, and only, member of staff that they are guaranteed to see every day. Having a clear check-in and check-out process allows important conversations to take place, to support a student's personal development.

A key part of a form tutor's role is ensuring that students are ready for the week ahead, or have had time to reflect before going home for the weekend.

How you carry this out is up to you – you could have students write things down, create form floor books or simply discuss.

Monday check in:

- Check timetables and discuss the week ahead. Ask students to show you their equipment and ensure they are clear about PE days, etc.
- Discuss any concerns for the coming week. Encourage them to rationalise and discourage catastrophising.
- Talk about things that they are looking forward to, and the steps they could take to have a positive week.

Friday check out:

- Look back on the week and celebrate successes (small and big).
- Take time to let students acknowledge and offload about what's not gone well, before encouraging them to let it go.
- Wish them a happy and safe weekend, and use this as an opportunity to remind them of any wellbeing or safety messages.

Taking it further

Have a form 'celebrate it' jar. Each week students write what they wish to celebrate on a slip of paper and place it in the jar. These can then be handed out at the end of each term or half term as a lovely way to celebrate success.

IDEA 56

Form identity

'We had such a laugh creating this, and it really helped my form to bond.'

Building strong relationships with your form is crucial, but so is them forming close bonds with each other. Form time PSHE discussions are a lot easier to navigate when your students are comfortable with each other. This idea is a fun and practical way to support this.

Before starting this activity, allow time for some easy getting-to-know-each-other activities. Keep this simple by using popular card and board games. This provides some much-needed warm-up time that will make the next stage easier.

Then move on to create a form motto or strapline. Share examples from well-known brands and organisations, unpicking what they like and don't like. Encourage all students to contribute adjectives and values that the form share, and then support them in putting these together into a catchy line.

Once you have your motto, it's time to move on to the form logo or crest. This is a chance to get their creative juices flowing! Again, show them well-known examples from brands, sports teams and universities. Encourage students to think about imagery that represents them, such as examples from their hobbies or faith, or logos from teams or bands that they love. Talk to them about colour psychology so they can think about this within their design.

Once you have created your motto and logo, display these with pride in your form room.

> **Bonus idea** ★
>
> To add some competitive energy, hold some awards, such as best motto, best teamwork, best innovation, most creative, etc. Forms could win cookies or similar.

IDEA 57

British values and assemblies

'Our assemblies enhance our citizenship curriculum.'

Schools must promote the fundamental British values of democracy, rule of law, respect and tolerance, and individual liberty. The citizenship curriculum in place this will take care of the knowledge and understanding of these values. Assemblies can be used to enhance this knowledge.

Use assemblies with a British values theme to emphasise the importance of the values, explore links to your school ethos and celebrate students who embody the values.

Use assemblies to explore how democracy is an ever-evolving concept, e.g. looking at the fight for suffrage, the life of Nelson Mandela or the 'Votes at 16' campaign. You could also lead assemblies introducing students to important campaigns and protests both in the UK and abroad, such as Black Lives Matter, #MeToo and the Youth 'Act Now' campaign.

When explaining the school's rewards and sanctions policy refer to the rule of law, such as the importance of fairness, equality and everyone understanding and benefiting from it.

Build the concept of respect into reward assemblies. Celebrate students who show respect to others, and also to themselves. Ask staff to make nominations and share their reasoning, or allow students to do so too.

There are many interesting assembly topics you could relate to rights, but a simple and often-overlooked one is linking student leadership opportunities to children's rights. Children have the right to have their views listened to, so when using assemblies to promote student leadership, make specific links to the Convention on the Rights of the Child.

Teaching tip

Think outside of the box when making links between British values, your school and topics that your students will find engaging. This brings British values to life and ensures the topic doesn't become a tick box for students to rote learn.

IDEA 58

Birthday bonanza!

'I learned so much about my form through doing this.'

Effective form time heavily relies on positive relationships. Having a day dedicated to each student within a tutor group is really special. It makes them feel valued and allows them to share something they love with their form group — it can be mutually beneficial!

Taking it further

If capacity allows, invite members of the wider staff body to share their birthday bonanza during form time. This could be face-to-face or online for the whole school.

As a form, design a calendar. Be creative with what this looks like. Each form member should create a 'pin' to represent them that is pinned to their birthday date. Pins might be a photo, their name, or a logo or picture that represents them — allow your students to decide.

Explain that on the school day closest to their birthday, they can have a birthday bonanza in form, which means they can choose a form time activity that represents their interests. Initially, students might keep this simple, e.g. playing their favourite card game.

Ideally, build this so that students feel comfortable sharing something that represents who they are. This might be playing their favourite song and explaining why they like it, or teaching their form a skill they have, e.g. how to say hello in a different language.

Build and model a culture of respect. Show genuine interest, ask questions and praise students for doing the same. Lead from the front too — when it's your birthday bonanza, share something with the form about yourself.

Part 7

PSHE ideas

IDEA 59

Writing on tables

'It felt strange at first, seeing students put pen to table, but now I promote it daily in my classroom.'

Hear me out! Allowing students to write on tables in PSHE can help them to feel safe and confident in recording how they feel. The non-permanency really encourages students to open up.

Teaching tip

If you have a floor book or similar, you could take photos of some of the tables as evidence (this can be anonymous).

Students writing on school furniture is something that has been a bane of teachers' lives for many decades. It can feel very strange to give students whiteboard pens and actively encourage them to write on your table, but the benefits are huge. Whiteboards are small but tables aren't, so students can write mind maps, extended sentences and large diagrams with ease on them.

This might sound glaringly obvious, but check two things first: are the pens definitely dry-wipe and not permanent, and are your tables smooth and non-porous? I advise a patch test!

Ground rules are key. Explain to students the rationale (to encourage confidence and support collaboration) and emphasise that they must follow your direct instructions: just because they can write on the table in your class, this does not apply to anywhere else in school unless directed by school staff.

Scenario-based activities are great for tables. Print out scenario examples and attach them to tables, then students can mind-map from this. Use a range of different colour pens to differentiate between ideas, e.g. green for positives and red for negatives.

Provide students with a damp cloth or wipes so that they can be in control of their table. This will also ensure students are equipped with the materials to clean the tables thoroughly at the end of the lesson, saving you time!

IDEA 60

Distancing techniques

'Talking about my personal feelings of what I would do in certain situations makes me feel uncomfortable.'

Remember that some students will have experienced the topics discussed in PSHE and may feel uncomfortable talking about what they would do in a given scenario. These ideas can help.

High-quality PSHE should assess students' ability to demonstrate skills such as empathy, maturity and decision-making across a range of likely situations, e.g. being offered drugs (see **Idea 82**). When facilitating this in class, we need to be mindful of their personal experiences.

Distancing techniques are just that: they distance students from a scenario by using made-up characters. Rather than asking 'What could you do in this situation?', teachers ask 'What could Sam do in this situation?'. Using made-up characters allows students to open up and feel safe (they are not talking about themselves), whilst still letting the teacher assess their knowledge, awareness and skills. Real-life scenarios involving celebrities work well for this. Teenagers may already be aware of some high-profile celebrity scenarios, so this can provide a rich discussion.

If the lesson is going well, and students are opening up, they could be brought into the scenarios as additional 'characters', e.g. 'What would you advise Sam to do?'. This still keeps the distance, as the focus is on the fictional Sam, but students can begin to talk about their personal ideas and views some more.

Even though distancing techniques help to depersonalise the topic, this does not mean that sensitive topics lose their need for sensitivity. Be aware of potential triggers and safeguard students accordingly (see **Idea 62**).

Teaching tip

When thinking up character names for your distancing scenarios, consider bias. Try to use gender-neutral names to encourage more open thinking.

IDEA 61

Coulda, shoulda, woulda

'I know the right answer for this one!'

PSHE encourages students to explore their moral compass, think about risk and navigate big life decisions. This idea gets students to unpick different options in PSHE-based scenarios, rather than giving you the answer they think you want to hear!

Quality PSHE should encourage students to consider how people might 'actually' respond in a given scenario, and why.

Begin by incorporating realistic scenarios that align with the safety message you are aiming to teach. For example, choosing a route to walk home when teaching about personal safety. Allow time for students to discuss the scenarios, but don't overly structure this as you want them to process the information freely depending on their lived experience.

Don't then jump to 'what they should do', which can feel like the next logical step. Instead, give students the tools to navigate the scenario in full.

Ask students what the person in the scenario 'could' do. Guide them in considering all the different options available. This supports students to think creatively and develop their problem-solving skills, allowing students to see that there are options within all situations.

Move on to 'should'. This will encourage students to consider the potential options and evaluate which might be the best and why.

End with what the person 'would' do. Is the person likely to do as they know they should? Or will they take another route? Why? This opens critical thinking discussions about peer pressure, managing risk and instinctual behaviour.

Taking it further

Share this method with your pastoral team. The 'could, should, would' model can be a fantastic tool when working individually with students who have made poor personal behaviour choices.

IDEA 62

Safeguarding against triggering content

'I feel safe in class because I'm informed about what's going on.'

PSHE deals with highly emotive and sensitive topics that can cause students to feel anxious or upset, as well as being potentially triggering for students who have lived experience of what's being taught. Preparing our students is vital.

To support and safeguard students they need to be aware of topics coming up and know how to ask questions and raise concerns. There are many simple steps that we can take to ensure students are informed and prepared.

Your PSHE curriculum will be mapped and planned. Use this to create a simple, stripped-back student version, and give this to students at the start of each term. This document should state the topics being taught, examples of the types of activities that will take place, and rough timescales. Talk through this with students and use this as an opportunity to remind them of the ground rules that will run alongside the topics being taught (see **Idea 63**).

Share this document with your pastoral and safeguarding teams before the topics are taught. If they know what's coming up in PSHE, they will be able to have one-to-one conversations with students who may find them difficult, and it will also pre-warn staff of any potential spikes in disclosures that may arise as a result of the topic being taught.

Be available to your students. Offer to talk through the curriculum with them after class if needed. This will rarely be taken up, but for some very nervous students this short conversation will remove their fears and allow them to take part.

Teaching tip

Drop in regular reminders about topics coming up, e.g. 'Don't forget, as outlined in your PSHE document, we will soon be moving on to the topic of consent, so pop and see me after school if you have any questions'.

IDEA 63

The power of opting out

'I'm teaching my students about boundaries and how to take care of themselves.'

Opting out can be seen as very much a no-go within education. As teachers, we are encouraged to ensure all students participate. Successful PSHE needs a climate where students are engaged but their boundaries are also respected.

Teaching tip

Ensure students are clear about what they can and cannot opt out of. Opting out is used to respect people's privacy and boundaries when discussing personal or sensitive information. It doesn't apply to generic PSHE work! Go through this at the start of each topic.

By letting students opt out, we can support them to opt in. Students can engage with learning without the fear that they will be made to answer a sensitive question in front of their peers. When meeting your PSHE class for the first time, collaboratively establish clear ground rules (see **Idea 64**), ensuring they cover the teacher's and students' expectations around answering questions in class. Ensure students understand the reasoning behind opting out. Explain that you are respecting their boundaries and that, in turn, they should respect yours.

Rather than cold calling, re-phrase the question as 'Would anyone like to tell me...?'. (There will often be at least one super-confident student in the class who is willing to share.) Then engage the rest of the class using thumbs-up/thumbs-down to gauge their opinions on what has been said, and summarise their answers.

Rather than using an agree/disagree activity where students have to move around the room and are visible, go for a head-down, thumbs-up approach. Students can contribute without being 'seen' and will therefore feel included in follow-up discussions, even if not wanting to speak.

Collate answers to questions by asking for them on sticky notes. These can then be collected up and summarised by you without mentioning any names.

IDEA 64

Establishing ground rules

'We have clear rules and expectations that are understood by all.'

Establishing ground rules isn't a new thing in PSHE, they've been a cornerstone of good practice for many years. We're revisiting ground rules here because too often they are presumed, glossed over or not respected. Examining your ground rules and looking at them through fresh eyes is never a wasted task.

Students need to understand that PSHE ground rules are different from school rules (although there may be some crossover) and the reasons for them. Remind students that PSHE deals with sensitive topics and that everyone, teacher included, needs to feel safe.

This should be done with students, not to them. Group them to brainstorm what they do and don't think is acceptable in PSHE lessons, collate responses and paraphrase these for them.

Once you have a range of ideas, look at each in turn and discuss why it's important and what the emotional repercussions could be if it wasn't followed. Students need to understand this and develop empathy toward other students.

If you would like to add any rules, suggest these to the class to consider. This helps with building a supportive team mentality, e.g. 'I would like to suggest..., what do you think?'.

Be clear about rules relating to confidentiality, from both a safeguarding and respect point of view. Go through with students, step by step, what could happen if they break confidentiality as well as your duty in passing on potential safeguarding concerns.

Revisit your ground rules frequently, and remind students about specific rules at key points, e.g. 'we are just about to discuss A, remember ground rule B, we said that...'.

Taking it further

Once you have a set of ground rules that everyone agrees with, print these off and sign them as a collective (you might need to print on A3 and then copy to A4). Keep a copy in the room and in the front of books. You could also share these with parents at consultation evenings.

IDEA 65

Reading in form time

'We're improving literacy and exploring PSHE at the same time.'

There are two things that many schools have in common: they want to improve literacy and they often struggle to find time in the curriculum for PSHE. So why not blend the two? A whole-school approach to form time reading, using carefully curated books with PSHE themes, can tackle both.

Teaching tip

Read to the class. This is the best way to support language development, as students learn from you how to read, e.g. correct tone, word emphasis and tempo. This will also ensure you keep pace. Ideally, do this under a visualiser so students can 'see' the words.

Staff buy-in is important. Ensure your CPD calendar reflects any training needed and involve staff in the planning process. For some staff, the thought of reading with, or reading to, their students may feel a little daunting – they need to feel supported.

When launching this idea, be specific about your reasoning. Explain how improving students' ability to confidently read will not only support them but will have a benefit across all curriculum areas, as students need a reading age as close as possible to their chronological age to be able to fully access exam content.

Form time slideshows need to be planned, provided in advance and easy to follow. You are asking teachers to go outside their comfort zone, so make it as easy as possible for them (this will also reduce kickback).

To keep things simple, use a text-per-term model so that each year group will read and discuss one book per term, three books a year. If this feels too large a task, reduce it, but working to a text per term will allow for greater coverage of PSHE themes. This also links nicely to the PSHE association core themes of Health and Wellbeing, Relationships, and Living in the Wider World, with each year group tackling one theme per term.

Create a working group to decide on the texts you will cover. These could be a range of fiction and non-fiction and should be challenging enough to expand vocabulary, but not so challenging that the students can't engage with them. Involve your staff body by creating an online form to gather suggestions. This helps staff to feel involved. You could even take suggestions from students.

Waterstones and some other bookshops have a great feature where you can search online for books that tackle certain themes across different age groups. This feature will help you with ideas for texts if you're a little stuck. It is highly advisable that all texts are read by a member of staff to ensure they don't cover very sensitive themes such as suicide or rape (it would be inappropriate to ask a tutor to tackle these).

Once you have decided on your books, it's time to get planning. Divide up the planning so that a different member of staff can plan for each text. If the task is down to one person or a very small team, start small and build, as this step can't be rushed.

Each book needs to be read, and whilst reading it, the member of staff should make a note of:

- new subject-specific words that might need unpicking
- parts of the book that lend themselves to inference
- parts of the book that lend themselves to a discussion.

Use these notes to build your slideshow, which should start with a picture of the book and some basic information. The class will then read through the book together, stopping at pages identified within the slideshow to explore a word, make an inference or discuss a theme. Ideally, aim for two whole-form activities relating to the text each week.

> **Taking it further**
>
> Encourage students to write book reviews, ideas for a 'second book' or come up with their own alternative endings.

IDEA 66

Shock tactics: wrong tactics!

'That will shock them!'

There is a PSHE myth still doing the rounds (and a mistake that I fell into myself when I first started teaching): 'if you show students shocking, gruesome and morbid pictures or case studies, you will shock them into making the right choices'. Wrong! There are better ways.

Taking it further

This information should be included in staff induction for anyone teaching PSHE as it's likely that some teachers will still see 'shock tactics' as good practice.

The myth is believable because employing these tactics in the classroom does get students' attention. They will listen intently, but what are you actually teaching them?

Shock tactics can do the very opposite of what we want them to. They can make students feel embarrassed and want to put their heads in the sand, or they can be so extreme that students can't relate them to their own experiences. There are more effective ways to educate young people to make informed decisions.

In RSE, don't use images to teach about STIs. Most STIs don't have visible symptoms, so this could do more harm than good in teaching students that 'mine doesn't look like that so I must be OK'. Or the images could make them feel so embarrassed about their sexual health that they refuse to seek help. Focus on developing confidence to discuss contraception and other prevention methods instead.

When teaching personal safety, don't show images of people that have lost a hand due to firework misuse, or talk about cases where someone has gouged out an eye through taking drugs. Young people perceive risk differently, and will likely react to such with a 'that won't happen to me' response. Instead, work on their empathy and ability to evaluate risk in these situations.

IDEA 67

Educating or glamourising?

'Woah! Look at his car, that's sick!'

When developing PSHE resources, it's easy to accidentally glamorise the exact behaviours and lifestyles that you are trying to educate against. Here's how to avoid that.

Teachers can fall into the trap of using imagery or examples from popular culture that they think will 'hook' the student's interest, but instead students end up more focused on the perceived glamour of the scenario, rather than the dangers. For example, a teacher might view a film about county lines as heartbreaking, as they might focus on the vulnerability, exploitation and fear shown. A teenager might view the film completely differently, only seeing the money, the power and the designer goods.

Don't remove all traces of money and status when delivering lessons on topics relating to gangs, exploitation and criminal activity, as these are genuine hooks that are used within the grooming process. But be aware of where they are represented within your units of work, and make sure your lesson plans reference how to approach these. For example:

- When showing cash made by drug dealing, discuss the realistic longevity of this. Explore the difficulties of spending 'dirty' cash, sentencing for similar crimes and the impact on future work and therefore earnings.
- When showing imagery of the latest phones and devices balance this with a discussion around what it might feel like to never be 'free' from your phone when in a gang situation.
- When images show high-cost items such as cars and watches, explore how it might feel to have to watch your back as someone will always be after what you have.

Teaching tip

Ensure you go through the session plans of any external visitors wanting to share their stories to educate. When done well, this is powerful, but when done incorrectly, this can turn someone's life story into a soap opera that students will love to hear, but learn little from.

IDEA 68

University links

'I couldn't believe how much the local university could offer!'

Engaging with universities is hugely valuable. Not only is it great for career education and raising aspirations, but it also opens the door for lots of peer/near-peer mentoring and education.

Each university will offer different things, so find out the contact details of the university director and head of student services and make yourself and your school known. Make it clear that you want to form a positive working relationship with the university and create mutually beneficial activities such as:

- **University visits:** This is mutually beneficial as it supports university applications and offers your students an aspirational careers visit.
- **Take-over classes:** Many final-year university students will be looking for work experience to add to their CV. Offer them the chance to run an introductory session to your KS4 students, e.g. third-year biochemists could take a Year 11 chemistry lesson.
- **Peer mentoring:** Many universities encourage volunteering as a part of their courses. Offer them a mentoring placement at your school. This provides your students with 'real models' and also supports the university.
- **Sexpression:** Sexpression is an independent UK charity empowering young people to make informed decisions about relationships and sex by training university students to run RSE workshops at local schools.
- **Streetlaw UK:** This is a programme in which law students plan sessions to deliver at local schools to educate young people about crime, the law and their rights.

Taking it further

Make up some school packs with your school prospectus, some goodies, your contact details and a cover letter, and take these to local university open evenings. Use these events as an opportunity to make your face known and get the conversations flowing.

IDEA 69

Recording learning

'Getting rid of exercise books is one of the most sensible decisions I have made.'

As it is not an exam-based subject, PSHE can have its challenges in terms of time, resources, and staffing. However, you have much greater flexibility on how you record students' learning. Here are some creative ideas on how to do this.

So much of PSHE learning is based around discussion work, role play and quality thinking time, but this can be difficult to evidence in a traditional exercise book. This can lead to teachers feeling stressed about 'lack of work', and encourages mindless copying from the board which benefits no one. With this in mind, re-think how you get your students to record their learning. If they write in exercise books because that's what all the other subjects do, ask yourself: is this the best way? PSHE time is scarce, so free up time to focus on what's important. Try these:

- Research PSHE floor books and adopt a similar model for your classes.
- Create a class reflection journal. Each lesson a different pair or group has the responsibility of reflecting on what they have learnt.
- Use a visualiser or tablet to take five pictures each lesson (of work, role plays, discussions, etc.), which are printed and kept in a class folder. Students take turns to annotate them.
- Keep to a traditional exercise book, but use it less frequently. For greater depth, ask students to mind-map what they think they know and want to learn at the start of a topic, with a full description of what they have learned at the end of a topic.
- If you're tech savvy, create a password-protected class blog, where everyone can upload photos and short videos to showcase the learning journey.

Taking it further

Reach out to your feeder primary schools and ask to see how they use floor books. This is a common primary model that often isn't used in secondary, but it's great for PSHE.

Part 8

Citizenship ideas

IDEA 70

Camera project

'This project helped me to think about what needs changing in my local area.'

This idea involves students taking photos of parts of their local area that they love, hate or want to change and communicating this to their local government. A great project for supporting active citizenship.

Taking it further

Invite your local councillors into school to visit your students, or ask if they would be willing to have an online meeting.

As this project involves students lobbying decision-makers, it is best delivered alongside citizenship topics such as local government, democracy or citizenship action.

In the classroom, group students depending on the ward in which they live. The 'Find your local councillors' page on gov.uk is a great way to open up discussions about what wards are and to see if your students know anything about their local government.

Show students a ward map (available online) and use this to explain the project to students. They need to consider what they love and hate about their ward and why, and also what ideas they have to improve their ward. Allow time for students to discuss this and make initial notes.

Introduce the cameras. Students need to take photo evidence to back up their ideas, e.g. photos of areas that look run-down, or where they think there is a need for better youth services. Explain that the photos will be shared with their local government as evidence.

Consider safeguarding requirements: students should not take photos of members of the public or enter places or areas in which they feel unsafe or are not allowed. Ensure each student signs a responsibility contract that outlines what they can and cannot do.

This should include looking after the cameras, personal safety, respecting other people's privacy, etc.

Inform parents of the project and ask them for any concerns they may have. This allows parents to support their children with the project, but also makes you aware of any potential issues, e.g. a parent might not want their child going near a notoriously busy road. Build this into the responsibility contract.

Once you have all the photos, it's time to get creative. Students may wish to make a poster, slideshow or video to display their findings. How much freedom you give them will depend on your curriculum time and the resources available. Ensure students are clear about the target audience – their local government. Their findings must clearly articulate what they love, hate or wish to change.

Package students' work and send it to your local councillors with a cover letter explaining the project. Provide your contact details and ask for a response. It's a good idea to post hard copies as well as email digital copies.

Reflect with the students about what they learned, what they enjoyed and how they could take this further. Remind them that communicating with local decision-makers is their democratic right.

> **Teacher tip**
>
> Think carefully about the type of camera you will use; you will need to consider cost, capacity and your school's safeguarding policy.

IDEA 71

Developing political literacy

'Once I got my head around some of the weird words, it all started to make a bit more sense.'

To support students in being able to take part in democratic processes, they need to understand and be confident with political terms. This idea tackles tricky terminology and is easy to implement as it's simply a change in the language used across the school. It might take a while for this to become habitual with staff, but once it has, job done!

Taking it further

Consider setting up your school council in a way that mimics the UK parliament (see **Idea 14**).

During school elections, use every opportunity available to use and teach keywords. Students should complete **manifestos** that are read by the **electorate**. If logistics allow, have a dedicated **polling station**, where students can complete a **ballot paper** and place it into a **ballot box**. Before the election, have **hustings** where candidates can **debate** in front of their peers, and allow for **canvassing**, where candidates can visit forms to speak to students. Teach what these words mean and keep using them.

School leaders should be collecting and listening to the student voice and use political terminology when doing so. Invite students to **surgeries** to discuss issues with key decision-makers. Consider using **referendums** to find out students' views about key decisions. This also creates a culture where students feel able to share their views responsibly and respectfully. Introduce the concept of **lobbying** and ensure they know they can do this.

IDEA 72

School surgery

'To effectively lead, I need to hear about our students' experiences.'

MPs hold regular surgeries for their constituents to meet them and share concerns. MPs also use them to discuss issues they have observed in their local area. Why not use this model? Enable constituents (students) to meet with decision-makers (school leaders).

The great thing about surgeries is that you have complete flexibility as to when they happen, how long they last and where they take place.

Clear parameters will be needed from the outset, covering what can be raised, how to pass information on and the next steps. School surgeries are for students to share ideas, thoughts and concerns about wider school life. They are less effective if used for students to complain about individual arguments.

Surgeries should be a place that is neutral and easy for students to get to, but that also offers a level of privacy. A free classroom near the canteen or a corner of the library works well.

Here are some options on timings:

- Multiple surgeries at the same time, once a half term/term. Each surgery has representation from a different area of school leadership.
- Weekly solo surgeries, e.g. Week 1: quality of education lead, Week 2: behaviour lead, etc.
- Hold surgeries as and when there's high need.

To ensure all students have the opportunity to attend, you could invite specific cohorts or forms at certain times, so you are not hearing from the same students repeatedly.

> **Bonus idea** ★
>
> Use your school administration teams or a trusted student school leader to support you with taking notes. The students' thoughts must be recorded and discussed during a SLT meeting.

IDEA 73

Citizenship in the wider curriculum

'This has helped to deepen our offer and allow students to see how citizenship is everywhere.'

Citizenship is a discrete National Curriculum subject and should have discrete time within the curriculum as such. But when this isn't quite possible, think wider. Are there links elsewhere?

With some strategic thinking you can find citizenship links in many areas. There are clear links to humanities and English, but less obvious ones elsewhere too. Be mindful that this may not cover the full citizenship curriculum but will enhance your offer.

Maths: Students can use percentages to evaluate loans, debts and investment returns, or analyse population data using census information, making future predictions.

Computing: Cover the importance of digital literacy and understanding mis-/dis-information at key times, such as in the run-up to an election or forming an opinion about global issues, e.g. immigration.

Technology: Refer to the global impact of the usage of certain materials, e.g. cotton, cobalt. Consider the impact of cost and availability of food as a result of changes in trade.

Art: Exploring the work of protest artists through the social values or concerns of the time, e.g. Banksy's anti-war imagery and critique of politics.

Science: Consider the legal implications for scientific advancement, e.g. cloning, IVF. Explore the role of scientists in advising government and global political organisations, e.g. during Covid-19 or tackling climate change.

Taking it further

Ensure you have time to meet with all your subject leaders. Ask them to bring their National Curriculum documents and schemes of learning and have the citizenship programme of study available too. Allow time to cross-reference and discuss where there is overlap. This can then be mapped out and recorded as evidence.

IDEA 74

Human rights club

'Attending this club has taught me so much, I feel proud of the impact I'm making to help others.'

Human rights is a core concept within citizenship. When exploring this topic, inequality regarding rights becomes apparent and your students might want to do something to address these injustices. Providing a safe space via a club allows students to learn more and make a responsible difference.

Consider who will lead it – you will have a range of staff keen to get involved. It's great for students to see that there are lots of different people who care about rights. Make it clear the club will be student-led and staff-facilitated. If staff take over by covering the inequalities that they are passionate about, this takes it away from the students.

Advertise the club alongside teaching the topic. This makes it less abstract and more likely that students will be prompted to join. If possible, consider having separate KS3 and KS4 clubs to explore topics in an age-appropriate way.

The first meeting should establish the ground rules and come up with a mission statement. Practise what you preach and include rights within this, e.g. everyone in the club has the right to freedom of expression, equality, etc.

Students will want to tackle a lot! Ensure decisions are made democratically. To allow adequate time, but also ensure there's range, run a year-long project alongside three termly or six half-termly smaller projects.

Set clear and realistic outcomes. This might just be to learn more; however, you could also educate others, lobby MPs, raise money or support national campaigns (Amnesty International has lots of ideas).

Taking it further

Don't become insular – share what you are doing with the rest of the school and the SLT.

IDEA 75

Active citizenship

'Our school provides chances for students to make a real difference.'

Quality citizenship includes active citizenship; this is clear in the curriculum and is a key feature on all citizenship studies exam boards. Give students the chance to be active citizens.

Teaching tip

The Association for Citizenship Teaching (ACT) has a wide range of easy-to-use student and teacher resources to support citizenship action.

Citizenship action is where students use their knowledge to tackle a citizenship issue and have an impact. It brings citizenship to life!

If we want to develop active citizens, we need to teach students how to carry out active citizenship, including primary and secondary research, and campaign methods, e.g. petitions.

It's also important that your school provides opportunities for students to develop the skills they will need to carry out citizenship action, such as teamwork, collaboration and respect.

Pre-planned citizenship action can be a simple starting point. Pick a scheme of work and build citizenship action into this. For example, if students learn about voting in Year 8, you could incorporate a 'Votes at 16' campaign alongside this, using ideas readily available online (ensuring you also allow students the option to campaign for the age to remain 18). This could be as simple as writing letters to your local MP or creating a display board. This also works well across curricula, so if Year 7 learns about climate change in science, plan your citizenship time to run a campaign alongside this.

Ensure students are realistic about endpoints and evaluate their actions by encouraging them to see the successes that they would otherwise miss, such as educating others or making local MPs aware of their concerns. Using pre- and post-action evaluation forms can support students in seeing their success.

IDEA 76

Human rights as a hook

'We use rights as our citizenship anchor; everything else stems from it.'

Trying to plan a citizenship curriculum when there is limited (if any!) discrete citizenship time on the timetable can be difficult. It can feel more manageable to create a curriculum based on human rights and tie your citizenship provision to this.

If you have a curriculum based on human rights then, even if you are using a combination of assemblies, parts of form time and the odd drop-down day here and there, it all still makes sense and doesn't feel disjointed to students. A human rights model can also link well to your school ethos and values and to British values. An example plan is given below.

Term 1: Human Rights

- KS3: The UK Equality Act 2010. Prejudice and discrimination.
- KS4: Global inequality. Reasons for migration, international organisations like the UN. Fair and free trade.

Term 2: Political Rights

- KS3: Introducing UK parliament and how we can get involved.
- KS4: Political campaign case studies in the UK and beyond.

Term 3: Legal Rights

- KS3: Introducing the UK legal system and our legal rights.
- KS4: Lawmakers and changers, exploring how and why laws change. International law.

Include the role of the media throughout and how this can have an impact, such as how the media reports on immigration or elections.

Teaching tip

The Association for Citizenship Teaching (ACT) has great resources designed for non-specialists. Parliament UK Education also has easy-to-understand videos and downloadable student booklets.

Taking it further

If following this model, KS4 lends itself well to opportunities for active citizenship (see **Idea 75**).

IDEA 77

Debate academy

'Can we have a debate this lesson?'

How many times do we hear students ask this? Students often love a debate, and this is great as it shows they are passionate about what's going on in the world and have an opinion that they wish to share. But do we teach this skill explicitly?

Teaching tip

Meet with your head of English to discuss potential collaboration. The development and use of oracy is a key part of language learning in the National Curriculum for English, and listening, speaking and debating also feature.

We would be wrong to presume that debating is an innate skill that teenagers naturally develop. It's a process that is massively dependent on what communication looks like at home, what they see and hear via the media, and how their friendship group tends to deal with heated discussion.

Teaching students how to debate respectfully and effectively is a core citizenship skill that will serve them well into adulthood, enabling them to advocate for themselves and others.

Build the debate academy into a specific scheme of work, and make this explicit to your students. They need to know that they are being taught effective debating skills so that they develop an awareness of this and can put it into practice.

Start by establishing conversation ground rules: what are you classifying as OK and not OK? Pick apart why it's not a good idea to shout, talk over people or swear during a debate. Explore the importance of remaining calm and dignified, and using an authoritative but respectful tone. Create your agreed-upon 'debate ground rules' and ensure these are displayed within the classroom.

Watch some real-life debate examples, and get students to identify what they think is effective and ineffective and why. Examples could include extracts from *Question Time*, or fictional examples such as the debate scene from *Clueless*. Just be sure to check for age appropriateness and access.

Explicitly teach the different aspects of a quality argument such as sentence starters, paraphrasing, using tone and pitch for effect, and so on. Model positive and negative examples of this.

When starting out, pick debate topics that are light-hearted. This allows students to practise what they have been taught without their emotions getting in the way. Topics that relate to them, but in a non-emotive way, work well, e.g. 'students should be able to have fizzy drinks in class'.

With these early debates, provide lots of immediate verbal feedback, and ask students to repeat and retry frequently. You could also set up groups whereby students observe each other and provide feedback.

Once you are happy that your students have mastered the technique of effective and respectful debating, you can move on to grittier debates, which will allow students to speak with passion, but in a considered way.

> **Taking it further**
>
> Once students have been through your Debate Academy, set up a debate club where different groups go head-to-head in a debate. These could be recorded and used to support future debate academies. You could even look into entering debate competitions.

IDEA 78

Five newspapers, one day

'This is a great little citizenship activity that also promotes literacy!'

Free press is a key element of citizenship education. It's important that students understand the concepts of media bias, misinformation and disinformation. Allowing time for students to compare and analyse newspapers supports this massively.

Teaching tip

This activity works just as well looking at old news stories (great as a secondary source for citizenship lessons!). Whenever you buy a set of newspapers, store these with your initial notes on key differences to use again. This will provide you with a bank of great resources to teach about free press and bias, as well as looking back on key news stories.

This idea will encourages students to pick out how different media organisations report on the same issue. It's also lovely to see students read a physical newspaper and engage with current affairs in this format, something they might not often get the chance to do.

This idea works best when there is a big news story to explore, such as a political scandal, global conflict or similar. In the morning, a staff member needs to buy five copies of different newspapers (more if you like), ensuring a mix of broadsheet and tabloid, and diversity in terms of the political spectrum. Students will need to have had prior teaching about free press and the role of the media.

In the classroom, place students into five groups, each looking at a different newspaper. Guide them for things to look for, such as headlines, front page images, style of writing, bias and general 'feel'. Encourage them to think critically about what they are reading, who it's aimed at and what the editor or reporter may have been trying to achieve.

Students should then rotate newspapers, carrying out the same activities each time. Encourage students to consider differences and similarities in how the same story is being reported by the different newspapers. Ensure you have looked through the papers yourself so that you can guide them with this.

IDEA 79

Engaging with power

'I can't believe I met them! They were nothing like I thought.'

Students need to understand that elected representatives represent them! Too often young people see local councillors or MPs as people that have an almost celebrity status and are in no way people that they can or should make contact with.

Effective citizenship should aim to break down these barriers and ensure that students can see themselves as a part of the democratic process, and where better to start than school?

Parliament UK Education offers free, curricular-linked interactive tours and workshops, which can take place in person or online. These run during autumn and spring terms and last approximately two hours. These award-winning sessions are very popular, so book in advance to avoid disappointment.

It is also well worth contacting your local MP and councillors, as many of them are very keen to get into schools to meet with young people. This is most likely to take place on a Friday during their constituency time. They could deliver an assembly, meet citizenship classes, or to really mirror democracy you could hold an open surgery (with teacher support).

'Learn with the Lords in School' is an opportunity provided by the UK Parliament, whereby a Lord or Baroness will visit your school to speak to students about their role. The visits take place on Fridays and run all year.

Taking it further

To ensure that these events happen, schedule them into your school calendar. Use dates such as UK Parliament Week or the Day of Democracy if you can.

IDEA 80

Me map!

'Our students loved finding their global links.'

This is a lovely activity to get students thinking about the global aspects of their identity.

Teaching tip

This activity relies on internet research, so be aware of misinformation, and support students to fact check and think about the sources of information. You could also pre-empt some common answers and have some initial answers ready.

This idea supports students in understanding how different traditions and cultures enrich their lives and how the world is interconnected.

Get students to write down their answers to questions about their identity, hobbies and favourite things, e.g. 'What is your favourite food?' or 'What are your top three hobbies?'.

Once students have lots of information about themselves, hand out A3 paper showing an outline map of the world. Explain that they are going to find out their global links, e.g. where their favourite genre of music originates. They will then find this country on the map and 'pin it' by writing a sentence or drawing a picture.

You could also include countries they would most like to visit, have already visited or have ancestral links to. If students aren't sure you could set this as an additional piece of homework to find out.

Students should end up with a map that is covered with things that relate to them. This is a great way of introducing topics such as globalisation, diversity and multiculturalism.

Part 9

Quality assurance

IDEA 81

What does the data say?

'How can you be sure your PSHE curriculum is doing what it needs to do?'

This idea will support you in ensuring your PSHE curriculum is data driven and personalised to the needs of your students.

Designing student surveys can be a difficult task to navigate, especially if PSHE is something that you are not yet completely confident with. Don't recreate the wheel! There are surveys ready and available for your school to utilise:

- The PSHE Association has downloadable pupil questionnaires for Key Stages 2–5 that ask students important questions relating to how much they enjoy PSHE, whether they find the lessons age-appropriate and how well they think they are progressing.
- For more detailed information about your students' perceptions of health and wellbeing, register for the My Health My School survey. This asks confidential, age-appropriate questions on eight PSHE themes, allowing schools to identify areas of need and compare their students' responses with national data.
- Explore online survey creators such as Microsoft Forms, Typeform or Google Forms to create your own student questionnaires, allowing you to unpick and investigate areas of your PSHE provision. These can be emailed to students or added to Google Classroom or Microsoft Teams.
- Meet with your pastoral team and DSL to discuss what the data is telling you and how the school can work collaboratively to meet needs, e.g. by adapting the PSHE curriculum, inviting guest speakers or working with specialist agencies.

Taking it further

Sharing anonymised information with local community partners may be a useful way of starting conversations and sharing good practice. For example, work with your feeder primary schools or local post-16 providers, community policing, local youth projects, etc.

IDEA 82

Assessing the right things

'How do I know if my students are doing well in PSHE?'

In PSHE students need to know information, but they also need to demonstrate the skills and qualities that will support them into adulthood — that's what you should also be assessing.

Decide on the key knowledge that students must know. Remember, they are not going to be sitting a GCSE in this subject, so think about it carefully. Students don't need to know the number of milligrams of alcohol per 100 millilitres of blood that constitutes drink driving, but they do need to know that drink driving is illegal. Think about the key facts that will help them to keep safe and make informed decisions.

- Teach this key knowledge and test it in the same way as you would for any other lesson, using recall strategies, multiple choice quizzes or a simple test. But keep it brief, focusing on the core knowledge that they *must* know.
- Then move on to the skills and qualities that align with this knowledge, and incorporate ways for students to demonstrate them, via scenario-based work, role play or personal reflections. If, for example, you have taught the key knowledge surrounding contraception and STIs, scenario-based work will allow students to demonstrate their understanding of how they could approach bringing up the topic of contraception with a partner.
- Be clear about the skills and qualities that you want to develop, e.g. confidence, empathy, informed decision-making and self-worth, and ensure your lessons allow students to demonstrate these.

Teaching tip

Encourage students to self-assess too. It can be powerful for students to see and acknowledge how their skills and qualities are developing through their PSHE education.

IDEA 83

Case studies

'It's lovely to look back at the students we have taught and the experiences they have had.'

Staff responsible for PD do a lot! However, it can be difficult to keep track of every opportunity and experience, and even trickier to highlight the impact of it all. PD case studies can help as they both evidence and highlight the great work you are doing.

Aim for quality over quantity. Select a range of students for your case studies – this is important as it will showcase how your PD offer develops all students.

Each case study should be a maximum of two sides of A4 – they're a snapshot, not a full report. Start with the student's name and basic cohort information, e.g. SEND, PP, EAL, etc.

The case study should give an overview of the different aspects of the PD programme they have experienced. You may wish to separate this into core, e.g. PSHE lessons, and non-core, e.g. interventions, etc. This will highlight the different journeys and experiences that students have engaged with.

Now for the important part: impact! A lot of this will be observational, but you could also refer to quantitative data that shows a positive impact, e.g. attendance data. Impact statements could include:

- **Student:** What do they think? How has the PD programme helped them?
- **Pastoral:** What observations has their head of year made?
- **Form tutor:** What impact has their form tutor witnessed?
- **Teacher:** Are there any teachers who have noticed a difference in academic progress as a result of the student's PD experiences?

Taking it further

If appropriate, reach out to parents to get an impact statement from them too. It would be great to explore how your PD programme is also making a difference outside school.

IDEA 84

External verification

'This gave me the confidence that I was on the right track but also provided lots of food for thought moving forward.'

It might seem strange to encourage (already very busy) school leaders to seek out external verification, but hear me out! From an inspection point of view, personal development is still in its infancy. External verification for PD can therefore be hugely supportive and helpful, providing leaders with clear next steps.

Going through external verification does two important things. It prepares PD leads by helping you to forensically analyse your offer and be better practised at showcasing this to others and, more importantly, it can provide you with lots of fantastic ideas on how to improve your school's PD.

External verification should never be completed in a silo, although the PD lead should oversee. Collating evidence should be a team effort, and this also helps the wider leadership and pastoral teams to better understand your school's PD programme.

External verification/awards you could explore:

- Young Citizens SMSC Quality Mark is a self-review tool that encourages leaders to assess their SMSC offer in depth.
- The Association for Citizenship Teaching (ACT) Quality Standard for Schools focuses on assessing your citizenship provision.
- The Quality in Careers Standard is the national quality award for career education, information, advice and guidance.
- UNICEF's Rights Respecting Schools Award.
- Stonewall offers the School Champion Award, covering school LGBTQ+ inclusion.
- There are also numerous school wellbeing awards, such as the National Children's Bureau Wellbeing Award for Schools.

Taking it further

If you are a part of a Trust, reach out to some other PD leads and consider going through verification together. This way you can practise with each other, be a sounding board and share resources. Some organisations also offer reduced rates for Trust completion.

IDEA 85

Market research

'Regularly speaking with our students helps me to triangulate our PSHE programme.'

PSHE will be explored in detail during an inspection. Key staff will be asked to discuss their rationale and curriculum documents, and students may be asked questions. Be ready! Ensure that triangulation is a termly part of your quality assurance.

PSHE doesn't have GCSE results to fall back on to prove its effectiveness, so to assure that your PSHE is meeting your planned intent, you are going to have to delve deeper. Speaking to students in a formalised way should play a key part in quality assurance.

The PSHE curriculum is broad so be strategic in what you quality assure and when. Start with statutory content first, as this will be a likely line of inquiry during an inspection.

Pick two year groups (one from each Key Stage) and look at the curriculum planning for the specific area you are focusing on. Discuss with the PSHE lead what students have learnt about this topic so far and the types of things they should be able to recall. Use student books to support these conversations.

Next, meet with a diverse group of students from each year group. If you looked at a student's work during your curriculum discussion, invite them to the meeting. Discuss with the students what they are learning. Keep to open questions and try to mirror the conversation you had with the PSHE lead. Hopefully what students say matches the curriculum and what you can see in books.

If there is a disconnect this will need to be unpicked further. Don't be alarmed if this is the case, as then it can be addressed.

Taking it further

As well as carrying out the qualitative market research, you could also email all students an online version of the questions to gather a larger snapshot of responses.

IDEA 86

Supporting non-specialists

'I've got PSHE on my timetable for next term, help!'

In an ideal world, PSHE would be a discrete lesson, planned and taught by subject specialists. However, we know that often it can fall to all content to be delivered in form time, or PSHE lessons can end up with anyone who is free at the time. How can these teachers be supported?

To ensure that PSHE is high quality, teachers delivering the content need to be comfortable, knowledgeable and supported. But this can be tricky when CPD time is tight and PSHE isn't their specialist area.

It's inappropriate to ask non-specialists to plan content for a sensitive topic that they are unfamiliar with, so if you don't have a PSHE lead planning centrally, consider using an 'off the shelf' resource such as Jigsaw PSHE, or using the PSHE Association programme builder.

Liaise with the SLT to find time for PSHE CPD that doesn't eat into staff's 1265 or take them away from subject-specific CPD, e.g. not attending assembly to free up a 20-minute PSHE catch up, or take them off break duty to attend a fortnightly PSHE coffee meeting.

Use Padlet, Teams or similar to set up an online CPD library. The key here is to keep things short, so bitesize articles or 5-minute videos work well. You could also use platforms such as Loom to create video walk-throughs of lessons coming up, to help non-specialists 'see' how the topic should be taught.

The PSHE Association offers lots of twilight CPD; if possible, give PSHE teachers an additional hour of PPA each half term (or more), on the condition that they attend specified courses. These could be from the comfort of their own home.

> **Bonus idea** ★
>
> Before each new topic, send teachers a quick online survey asking them to rate their confidence and state how they would like to be supported. When time is tight, it is ideal to be able to provide individual teachers with the exact support they need in a way that suits them.

IDEA 87

Fact-checking and relevance

'Nothing ages a PSHE teacher like hearing a collective "cringe" from a rowdy class of teenagers!'

PSHE resources need to be factual, accurate and relevant. Due to the nature of the content, they can age quite rapidly and a once modern and engaging stimulus can quickly be viewed as cringeworthy by critical teenagers. Reviewing is vital!

Teaching tip

Sometimes, looking at resources through fresh, non-teacher eyes can uncover issues you hadn't even noticed. If you have teenagers in your family, use them! Get them to look over some of the resources and give you honest feedback.

Quality assure resources annually. This does not mean that changes need to be made each year, but looking at resources through fresh eyes will uncover tweaks necessary to ensure the resources continue to be high quality.

Create a checklist for each unit of work – this will keep the quality assurance focused and will hopefully speed up the process.

Be factual and accurate. Laws change, so the PSHE resources need to keep up. Make a note of the units of work that reference laws and add these to your checklist. If you have a Safer School Officer/PCSO, ask for their support in checking laws are up to date.

Be relevant. When using a stimulus in PSHE lessons this needs to be relevant to a teenage audience. For example, do you have lessons that refer to Facebook, when most of your students view this platform as old-fashioned? Do you use slang in scenarios that has lost its meaning or is simply not used by teenagers today? Your checklist should prompt you to look out for these and update them.

Use your school leadership groups. Ask them to be your 'second eyes' and look over aspects of resources and feedback their thoughts to you. As they are not teachers, keep their quality assurance bite-sized and focused, e.g. feeding back on a particular scenario resource or video.

IDEA 88

Positively inclusive PSHE

'We ensure that all students are "seen" within our PSHE curriculum.'

How inclusive is your curriculum? When talking about inclusion in this sense, we are not just referring to teaching topics such as different types of family or discrimination; we're thinking about what the students 'see' within their curriculum.

This will involve scrutinising your curriculum and checking for bias, as well as ensuring that protected characteristics are well-represented. Initially, this might mean going through your current resources, making tweaks where necessary, and then in future ensuring all your units of work are positively inclusive.

Look through scenarios and case studies, thinking carefully about the identity of the characters and unconscious bias that these could display. Where possible, use gender-neutral names, particularly in case studies focusing on romantic relationships.

Consider common stereotypes when using imagery to represent careers and ensure examples show a mixture of different identities representing different areas of work. Pay particular attention to areas where we know there are gaps, such as women in STEM.

Do your resources refer to and show people who have a disability? (This should not be limited to just teaching on the topic of disability discrimination.) For example, in a group of friends, one might use a wheelchair or might have a visual impairment.

Likewise, when referring to case studies looking at families, are you referring to blended, multi-generational and single-parent families? Are you showing single parents, adoptive parents and same-sex parents?

Taking it further

Don't forget to quality assure any external speakers too. You need to be sure that they are not biased, and that their values around inclusion mirror that of your school.

IDEA 89

Let's talk about sex! (Unless we can't?)

'I'm constantly worried that a class discussion will turn to sex.'

When changes to statutory RSE were made in 2021, this was both a blessing and a curse for PSHE leads. It's great that the subject was given more prominence, but legal opt-out for sex education has made teaching the statutory for all relationship content complex. How can you tackle this legally and sensitively?

Teaching tip

Once RSE identification has been completed, ensure that the document is shared with the SLT for final approval, and to support their understanding of this key area of policy.

Sometimes the division between sex and relationships is clear, but often it's not. A lesson on different types of relationships can turn into a discussion about sex if a student asks how same-sex couples have sex, for example.

This idea talks you through an approach that supports dividing the two, without silencing students from asking important questions.

First identify which of your PSHE lessons are about sex, which are about relationships, and which are about sex and relationships. You need a team of people to do this as a range of different opinions is key. Create a simple table that highlights the year group, topic title and lesson title, and then identifies if the lesson is sex, relationships, or sex and relationships. You might find it useful to refer to the PSHE association programme of study to help you.

You will likely find that most lessons fall into the relationships category, and that there are only a handful that are very clearly sex education. To keep the relationship lessons available to all students, there needs to be a clear strategy for when a student asks a very sex-specific question during a lesson that has been identified as relationship-based.

Introduce the 'park it' board. In each PSHE classroom, ensure there is a pinboard and stash of sticky notes. During a relationships lesson, if a question is asked that is very sex-specific, and you have students in the classroom whose parents have legally withdrawn them from sex lessons, 'park' the question. Write it on a sticky note, and stick it to the board, ensuring you thank the student for their question and assuring them it will be answered soon.

When it's time for the lessons that you have identified as sex education, ensure you refer back to your 'park it' board and answer the questions that have been asked in previous lessons. This ensures that students receive the answer they want, that you are protecting yourself legally, and that students who have been withdrawn from sex lessons are not made to feel uncomfortable or singled out.

This also helps to keep your relationship lessons focused. Students will feel heard and respected, but the lesson will also stay on track as per your curriculum document. It is vital that all staff teaching PSHE know which lessons are identified as relationships, so they know to 'park' any sex-specific questions – this should be a key feature of department meetings.

> **Taking it further**
>
> Ensure this curriculum document is shared on your school website. This will have taken a lot of work, so share it! This will also provide parents with valuable information about your RSE curriculum.

IDEA 90

Vetting external agencies

'If I'm putting someone in front of my students, I need to know they are decent.'

It's very common to reach out to third-party people when delivering your school's PD programme. A wide range of organisations advertise their services to come into school to deliver an assembly or workshops. If reaching out externally, quality assurance is vital to ensure alignment with your values.

Don't be put off external delivery, students often enjoy hearing from different adults, and they can be a huge support when delivering specialist areas of the curriculum. Following these simple steps will ensure a high quality experience:

- Ask around and use social media to request recommendations.
- Always ask for resources before delivery so they can be quality assured.
- Carry out a social media search of the organisation or speaker, ensuring you are looking beyond the first set of results.
- Be wary of organisations or individuals offering their services for free – there may be no bad intention but always check for signs of potential indoctrination or lack of balance.
- Where possible, ask for the names of schools that can give a reference rather than simply relying on what is on their website.

Taking it further

Alongside your safeguarding policies regarding external visitors, ensure you have a clear policy regarding external speakers – this will ensure that all staff remain vigilant when making external bookings.

IDEA 91

Evidencing your PD via data

'We might not have GCSE attainment data, but we do have data!'

Much of the evidence will be within your school culture — how students interact with each other and how your school 'feels'. A positive culture is palpable. But don't forget to use data too.

Having numbers and statistics helps you to become more strategic. Data shows you what's working well and where there are concerns so you can put resources where they are most needed and will have the most impact.

Identify days when attendance dips. Could you organise a fun PD activity to take place during this time? Could you develop a collaborative rewards trip for improved attendance, bridging attendance and cultural capital? Could you encourage students with low attendance by asking them to become members of a leadership group? Track attendance data prior to, during and after PD interventions to assess their impact.

Work with your behaviour team to examine trends relating to negative sanctions and then tackle this specifically within your PD programme. Following specific interventions, does the sanction data decrease?

Don't forget reward data. Look at points within your PSHE curriculum where values such as respect and empathy are specifically taught. Can you see an increase in reward data from students who have taken part in these sessions?

Track different elements of your Year 11 destination data. Which post-16 opportunities are growing in popularity? How many of your alumni are going onto level 4 or 5 courses? Does this correlate with programmes you have within the school, such as careers in the curriculum approaches or visits to FE or HE providers?

Taking it further

East Learning provides a range of school packages that collect student data, advise on interventions and assess the impact of your PD programme.

Part 10

Whole-school approaches

IDEA 92

Knock, knock

'Your door is the entrance to your classroom. What does it say about you?'

Students pass through many doors during the school day. Most won't give it a second thought — why would they? However, a classroom door is a clear boundary, separating the hall from a shared teaching space. Use these doors to celebrate identity, recognise role models and provide PSHE information.

Taking it further

The school is a community, so get everyone involved! Think about using the doors to office spaces, kitchens, sports halls, etc. to spread your whole-school PD messages.

This approach works best if everyone takes part. Decorate the school with a wide range of inspirational door signs.

A4 snap frames make displaying posters much easier — they look neat, make changing signs easier, and are relatively cheap to buy. If you have a marketing team in school, ask them to produce templates that all staff can use.

Make the most of key weeks and months pertinent to PD, e.g. Pride, Black History Month or International Women's Day. Ask all teachers to print a picture and description of a role model from this specific community.

Role models don't have to be famous. If staff feel comfortable, sharing a family member or friend who is an inspiration works well too; we all know how much students like to know a little more about us!

Door signs can also be used to promote a wellbeing strategy in school, such as displaying wellness and mindfulness tips on each door during exam season or suggestions for New Year's resolutions in January.

PD and literacy can both be supported by displaying the front cover of your favourite book and why you like it. If many books are displayed this will inspire students and develop cultural capital.

IDEA 93

Wall of fame

'It's by far my favourite part of the school.'

Publicly celebrating the achievements of your cohort is a fantastic way to raise aspirations, develop self-confidence and award extra-curricular activities.

When students move from primary to secondary, collective celebration can become lost, or reserved for award assemblies. A wall of fame provides students with a reminder of all the great things that students are doing both in school and in their personal lives.

Choose a large space for your display, and have fun with how it looks. Encourage students to come up with a design theme, e.g. the Oscars. You want students to be happy to have their photo displayed on the wall. If initially they are reluctant, just display their name or ask them to choose an image that represents them.

Include the more traditional awards on your wall of fame, e.g. subject awards, but also think creatively to celebrate a wider range of success.

Consider your core values and celebrate students demonstrating these. This is also a great way to celebrate improvement and perseverance.

Ask staff who run extracurricular clubs to nominate students, e.g. for 'player of the match' or the 'best baked Alaska'. Aim for a wide range, and get photos if possible.

Ask form tutors to nominate students who have achieved things outside of school, such as gaining a black belt in martial arts or a graded exam in music. Develop a celebratory culture where students want to be on the wall and come directly to staff to share achievements.

Bonus idea ★

To encourage a celebratory culture, consider attaching a reward linked to appearing on the wall, both extrinsic, e.g. points, and intrinsic, e.g. by verbally congratulating the student.

IDEA 94

Yours sincerely

'I love reading the different signatures. It makes a very normal part of the job feel special.'

Emails are a necessary part of school life and students may use them frequently to contact teachers and ask questions about their learning. Make them count!

With emails going backward and forward, why not use this as an opportunity to share PD messages within your email signature? These could be changed every month, or every half term, to keep them fresh and to align with a school PD theme or national/global campaign.

Ideas for email signatures:

- The current book you are reading.
- A quote from an inspirational person, which could be aligned with Pride Month, Black History Month, etc.
- A place that you would love to visit and why.
- A person who has gained your respect and why.
- Something you would change about the world.
- Top tips for study and wellbeing, which could be aligned with exam season.
- Your proudest moment.

Email signatures should be short and snappy. A sentence or two is ample; any more and they will look clunky. Create some basic examples for staff to use for inspiration.

Taking it further

If launching this idea with staff, use this as an opportunity to revisit your email protocol in terms of wellbeing, e.g. expectations around when to send emails. Allow staff to opt out of personalised email signatures if they feel uncomfortable.

IDEA 95

PD parent evenings

'We reframed our thinking. Parent evenings are no longer just about supporting students with their learning, they also support families with student personal development.'

Parent evenings are a common feature of school life, often focused on student achievement and outcomes. Why not provide parents with information about the personal development of their children too?

Consider hosting PD parent evenings, where parents can meet the wider staff body and gain information and guidance about their area of expertise:

- **Careers evenings:** A chance to hear from the careers manager and meet the wider team. Ideally, it would be great to invite local college and sixth forms to this evening too, and have representation from the National Apprenticeship Service, the National Citizenship Service, etc.
- **Safeguarding:** A chance to meet with the safeguarding and pastoral teams to look at issues facing young people and seek advice about how they can better support them.
- **Online safety:** This is such a huge issue that you might decide to host this as a discrete event. The computing lead, pastoral and safeguarding teams could offer advice concerning online safety.
- **Exams and wellbeing:** This event could be hosted by pastoral teams and subject leads, giving practical advice on how to support young people who are studying for exams, both from an academic and wellbeing perspective.

Taking it further

You could look at exploring a blended approach. This is particularly useful if you struggle to get families in for parent evenings. Whilst a traditional parents' evening is taking place, host a PD parent event in a room nearby. This way, parents can take part in both on the same evening.

IDEA 96

Parent support group

'We ensure our parents are fully engaged in school life.'

The transition from primary to secondary is a big step for parents as well as students. Suddenly their children are taught by lots of different teachers and engaging in different experiences, and there is a wide range of policies, which can all feel alien. Offering a parent support group can counteract this.

Teaching tip

To keep momentum, host a sign-up stand at Year 7 consultation evenings. New parents will likely be keen to get involved and be a part of the group.

A support group allows staff to update parents with key information, seek their views and better engage them in school life. The group doesn't replace consultation evenings but provides an additional layer of communication.

Establish a core team to oversee the group. Ideally, this should include someone from each area, e.g. behaviour, SEND, quality of education, and so on. It would also make sense for parent governors to be involved too.

Be clear about the aims and parameters of the group – this needs to be manageable and have clear boundaries. A workable model is a termly online meeting and a half-termly informative email/newsletter and online survey.

Calendar your online meetings in advance, ensuring the core team take it in turns to plan and lead. Keep meetings short – 45 minutes is ample. Share the upcoming meetings calendar with parents when they sign up.

Launch the group via a text message to parents, outlining the aims of the group, with a link to fill in their email address if they would like to be added to the distribution list. Ask your admin team to create the list (ensure you are clear in your launch text that this will be happening). This list can then be used for all communication and makes inviting parents to online information meetings quick and easy.

IDEA 97

Shout about it!

'Our display boards serve a purpose that goes beyond simply looking good.'

Most schools have display boards on their corridors. Sometimes it's useful to step back and consider who these are really for.

Think about what you have on the walls in your own home. If you surround yourself with things that inspire you, and make you feel good, why should schools be any different?

If you use display boards to inform students about a topic, consider including tear-off strips, giving a useful website or similar, that students could take home. Or, if your school allows phones, display QR codes that link to websites with more information.

Use your walls as an opportunity to showcase local artists, culture celebrations and traditions. Displays don't always have to be related to school activity, they can be a way to link your school to its local community and provide cultural capital.

Don't limit students' art to the art rooms and corridor, use it all over. Your art teachers will have masses of work that has been created by students over the years, display this! This will grab students' attention and inspire them a lot more than displays relaying instructions.

Photo displays are a great way of celebrating school activities that can truly capture the essence of your school. Although there's nothing wrong with posed photos, the images that capture moments of awe and wonder can often make more vibrant displays and create a feeling of excitement whilst conjuring up fond memories, such as school trips, prom and reward days.

> **Bonus idea** ★
>
> Numerous graffiti art organisations work with students to create individual or group pieces, both on boards to display indoors as well as large-scale group pieces to cover outside walls. They work with students to create art that aligns with school values.

IDEA 98

PD student score

'We discuss holistic development with our parents.'

Build a culture where PD scores are shared and celebrated alongside attainment scores.

Parent evenings and written reports are an opportunity for parents to find out about their child's attainment and current grades. Make sure you are reporting on a student's personal development too.

Develop a whole-school PD score for each student, which could then be shared with parents to inform them of how well their child is engaging in additional opportunities, PSHE lessons and demonstrating positive character attributes, amongst other things.

Ideally, the PD score would be developed in collaboration with your wider staff body. Experts within key areas need to give their input, and a scoring system needs to be agreed. You could keep things simple by using an Emerging, Expected and Exceeding scale (similar to primary), or break it down so that the score is more granular, as per the illustrative example below, which is based on an agreed number score for the Extra-curricular section and a measure of attitude for the Form time section.

Consider which factors you will take into consideration, and what each score looks like. This could be related to a set, agreed number, or based on attitude and willingness. The table on the following page gives two examples. An editable version of this example scorecard is also available in the online resources for this book.

> **Taking it further**
>
> Alongside each score, consider what information you could provide to parents to help them support their children at home, e.g. a copy of your school extracurricular timetable, or information about the UK Youth Parliament.

	Emerging	**Expected**	**Exceeding**
Extra-curricular	Attends 1–5 opportunities per half term.	Attends 6–10 opportunities per half term.	Attends more than 11 opportunities per half term.
	Takes part in at least 3 special events each term.	Takes part in at least 3 special events each term.	Takes part in at least 5 special events each term.
Form time	Complies with form time activities.	Shows good engagement with form time activities.	Shows consistently excellent engagement with form time activities.
	Occasionally contributes own ideas and takes part in discussions.	Often contributes own ideas and takes part in discussions.	Always contributes own ideas and takes part in discussions.

These are illustrative examples; it is up to your staff body what these scores should look like.

IDEA 99

Supporting new students

'This helped me to get to know my school and work out what goes on in it.'

Being a new student can be daunting. Aside from new friendship groups, it can also be challenging to understand how PD works, who all their new key people are and the opportunities available to them. Take a step back and consider how you are supporting new students.

Taking it further

With a tiny bit of tweaking, this guide to PD could also be used for new staff, ensuring they are supported in understanding how PD works at your school and their role within this.

Each school will have a unique approach to PD. Schools use different names for PSHE, the role of the form tutor can vary, and the extracurricular offer can be poles apart from what students were used to at their previous setting. Producing a 'Guide to PD' leaflet can be a huge support.

Keep the guide simple – one double-sided sheet is ample and should be more than enough space to fit key information.

Your guide could include: form time expectations and the role of the form tutor; what your school calls PSHE and when and how this is delivered; the different leadership streams you have and who to contact to find out more or apply; your extra-curricular timetable and how to sign up; details of your basic careers offer and where the careers manager is based.

From a safeguarding and pastoral point of view, the guide should also include the photos, titles and roles of key staff within this area, as well as information about how the student can raise a concern or seek advice.

IDEA 100

Policy makers

'Our policies impact our whole school community, so we consult our whole school community, including our students.'

Policies exist to ensure that schools are following the very best practices across a range of areas and that students and staff are kept safe. Why not involve students in the process? They are stakeholders too!

More often than not, school policies are written by a small number of school leaders and then shared with wider stakeholders to implement within their practice. These policies directly impact students, but students are not always involved in their creation.

First, be realistic about student involvement. Schools have a multitude of policies, some of which will have little interest to young people, so focus on the ones that students better understand and feel the impact of, such as teaching and learning, behaviour, attendance, and so on.

Gather student contributions in a young person-friendly way, and set up focus groups whereby the policy writer can meet with several students to gain their insight into that particular area of school life.

Consider bringing policy contributions into student leadership streams, if you have a leadership group that looks at rewards, involve them in contributing towards your behaviour and rewards policy.

When key policies are written, inform students of these in assembly (in a young person-friendly way). If students are aware of the existence of policies and their importance, this makes discussions around enforcing them much easier.

Bonus idea

Work with your young people to create student versions of the school policies that impact them. Policies are often written for an adult audience—making them accessible to your students is vital if you wish for them to be referred to and understood.